# What they don't te

# ART

I LOVE YOU.

## By Catherine Charley

### Illustrations by Bob Fowke

Dedicated to art lovers everywhere.

*Hodder
Children's
Books*

a division of Hodder Headline plc

Hello, my name's Andy Craft. I'm an art student.

And I'm *Olive Green*. I'm an art student too. Is your knowledge of art a bit sketchy? Come with us and we'll open your eyes to the amazing world of art.

Unfortunately it is impossible to mention by name everyone who has helped with this book, but the author and publishers would particularly like to thank Joseph McBrinn for his support and advice.

Text copyright © Catherine Charley 1998
Illustrations copyright © Bob Fowke 1998

The right of Catherine Charley to be identified as the author of the work and the right of Bob Fowke to be identified as the illustrator has been asserted by them in accordance with the Copyright, Designs and Patents Act 1988.

Produced by Fowke & Co. for Hodder Children's Books

Cover: PW191677 Composed Head (tissue and oil on canvas) by Bona (b. 1926) Private collection, Paris/Peter Willi/Bridgeman Art Library, London/New York. We have been unable to trace the copyright holder but if notified we should be pleased to amend the acknowledgements of any future editions.

Published by Hodder Children's Books 1998
0340 713305

10 9 8 7 6 5 4 3 2 1

Hodder Children's Books
a Division of Hodder Headline plc
338 Euston Road
London NW1 3BH

Printed and bound by Clays Ltd, St Ives plc
A Catalogue record for this book is available from the British Library

# CONTENTS

 Watch out for the *Sign of the Foot*! Whenever you see this sign in the book it means there are some more details at the *FOOT* of the page. Like here.

# WHAT IS ART???

SO THIS IS A BOOK ON ART? BUT WHAT IS ART?

SCULPTURES, ARCHITECTURE, TAPESTRIES, PAINTINGS,

TOTEM POLES, LACE-MAKING, PHOTO GRAPHS.

A COMIC STRIP. US IN THESE DRAWINGS.

WELL, WHAT CAN BE CALLED ART IS OFTEN A MATTER OF OPINION.

SO WHAT IS ART FOR?

TO CREATE EMOTIONS, FOR MAGIC, RELIGION, TO DECORATE, TO EXPLAIN THINGS, TO RECORD THINGS, TO TELL STORIES, TO MAKE PEOPLE LAUGH, TO MAKE PEOPLE THINK, TO PERSUADE PEOPLE TO DO SOMETHING, FOR ITSELF, FOR THE ARTIST, FOR THE PUBLIC...

I BEGIN TO SEE...

You can't have a piece of art without an artist.

But there is no agreement on who can call themselves an artist!

Every piece of art has a little bit of the artist in it.

At different times and in different places, artists have been regarded as the lowest of the low. At other times and in other places they have had great influence.

Owning certain pieces of art can give people importance in their own society.

An artist is always influenced by something, even if he or she reacts against it.

The artist's finished piece is influenced by what she or he makes it from, for example paint and paper, bone, wood, marble, skin, rope, rice ...

What one person thinks of as beautiful, another person thinks of as ugly.

Art has had different purposes at different places and at different times. Very seldom was the art that you see in galleries and museums originally meant to be there.

What you as an individual think about a piece of art depends on where and when you live and on your own experiences and knowledge.

## READ ON TO FIND OUT ABOUT ...

Just about anything and everything! Obviously all the art from all the world from the very dawn of time can't be described - but we can give you an idea of the story of art from its beginnings to the present day ... Prepare yourself for some surprises!

# VERY EARLY ART

## HOW IT ALL BEGAN ...

## A QUICK DASH TO THE PAINT SHOP FOR A CAN OF PAINT ...

Well, no actually. Artists had to make the paint themselves. Mostly they used different coloured earth or clay - red, yellow, brown or green. This powder, known as *pigment*, was then mixed with other things - egg white, animal fat, plant juice, blood, urine...

## AND A PAINT BRUSH ...

This was a bit easier. You could make brushes out of feathers or by tying animal hair to the end of a small bone. Or sometimes you might reckon just a stick or even a finger was better. A slightly wilder alternative was blowing the paint on to the wall of the cave through a hollow reed. Pads made from moss, leaves or animal skins were pretty efficient too. If you wanted to make sure your outlines were clear you might have used a sharp stone. All in all, quite a lot of choice!

 Black paint was made from charcoal, which is wood burnt in an airtight container. Artists still use charcoal today.

8

## VERY EARLY CAVE PAINTINGS

### LASCAUX I - A REAL CAVE IN FRANCE FULL OF VERY, VERY, VERY OLD PAINTINGS.

Some of the most famous early cave paintings in the world were found by some boys at Lascaux in France in 1940 when they lost their dog, Robot. They heard him yapping, and followed him down the hole he had fallen into. This proved to be the entrance to a wonderworld of horses, bison and other animals painted on the walls of a huge underground cavern! Those who claim to know these things reckon that these paintings were created about 15-20,000 years ago.

### LASCAUX II - A PRETEND CAVE IN FRANCE FULL OF VERY, VERY, VERY NEW PAINTINGS - WHAT?!

Lascaux II is a copy of the paintings in the main cave at Lascaux I! Despite the fact that the paintings in Lascaux I had existed for thousands and thousands and thousands of years, when tourists were allowed in to look at them, they began to deteriorate.

Literally the "hot air" of people's breath made the cave damp. Lascaux I was only open from 1948 to 1963. Now if you go to look at the paintings you see them in the specially built Lascaux II - a few minutes' walk away from the original cave.

 ## ALTAMIRA - A VERY DRY CAVE IN SPAIN WITH SOME MORE VERY OLD PAINTINGS FOUND IN EUROPE.

These paintings are believed to be 13,000-20,000 years old and they were found in the 19th century. They were some of the first cave paintings to be discovered in Northern Europe and were so well preserved by the dry atmosphere that at first they were thought to be fakes. "How," said the critics, "could anyone so long ago have created something that was so real?"

But they did, and not just in Spain. Ancient cave art has been found in *North Africa*, *South America* and also **AUSTRALIA:**

 ## HUNTING SCENES:

On the north coast of Australia some of the Aboriginal artwork is believed to be 20,000, or even more, years old. These pictures are also of hunting scenes with animals being chased by stick-figure hunters, all drawn with red-ochre.

---

 *Red-ochre* is natural red coloured earth which is used as a pigment for painting.

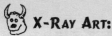 **X-Ray Art:**

Thousands of years later (but still thousands of years before today - probably about 9,000 years ago, in fact) Aborigines in north Australia were doing "X-ray" pictures. These were sort of see-through pictures - they showed what freshwater animals looked like under the skin. Often of fish, turtles, geese and crocodiles the pictures showed not only the skeletons of the animals but also their internal organs, including intestines, heart and lungs. Yuk!

## But why did all these people paint so many animals?

Maybe they were influenced by magic or religion, or a mixture of both. Some of the animals in the caves in Lascaux and Altamira have spears or arrows pointing at them. The people who lived at this time were hunters and perhaps they believed that, if, before a hunt, they painted the animals they wanted to catch they would have success on the expedition. Some of the paintings are just done on top of each other without any apparent regard for the ones underneath - this gives a further suspicion that they were done as part of a "Good Luck on the Hunt" ceremony.

## Very Early Sculptures

But people weren't just hanging around in caves painting, they were also making sculptures. Two little statues that survive from central Europe are the 11.5 cm high limestone *Woman from Willendorf* (Austria) and the 20.3 cm tall ivory *Man from Brno* (the modern Czech Republic). Both of them are probably about 25,000 years old.

11

# Ancient Art

## BUT NOT AS ANCIENT AS 'EARLY'

Not just paintings and sculptures, but buildings, tombs, jewellery and furniture too!

## INCREDIBLE FACTS ABOUT SOME ANCIENT STRUCTURES (WHICH YOU CAN STILL SEE TODAY)

**Newgrange** (in Ireland)

This is an incredible 5,000-year-old tomb which was built even before the pyramids. It's a man-made mound (a massive 9 m at its highest part and 103 m in diameter) standing in fields overlooking a river valley. The stone workmanship of these early people was incredible. A long passage leads to a high (6 m) round room in the centre. Spirals, zigzags and circles are carved on most of the stones in this chamber.

In fact, no bodies, or evidence of bodies have been found, so no one actually knows if Newgrange really was a tomb as such. Maybe it was kept as a special place for important dead people to lie with the spirits until they were buried somewhere else. There is evidence of about forty structures like this in the river valley.

## The heaviest building in the world

The heaviest building in the world is probably *still* the Great Pyramid in Egypt. It is said to be made of over two million limestone blocks, each weighing at least two tonnes. It covers a huge area. The Great Pyramid was built about four and half thousand years ago as a tomb. The chambers inside all face west, the direction where the Ancient Egyptians believed the Land of the Dead was.

## Ziggurats

Ziggurats were enormous temples made of terraces of mud brick in what is now Iraq. They were built about 4,000 years ago in the middle of the first cities of the world by people called the Sumerians. In fact everything was built of mud brick in these cities as that's the only building material they had. One of the most important of these cities was called Ur. The ziggurat of Ur was 30 m high and dedicated to Nanna, the Sumerians' god of the Moon.

## The Palace of Knossos on Crete

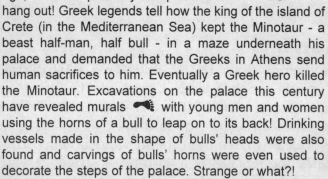

If you were into worshipping bulls about three and a half thousand years ago, this was probably the place to hang out! Greek legends tell how the king of the island of Crete (in the Mediterranean Sea) kept the Minotaur - a beast half-man, half bull - in a maze underneath his palace and demanded that the Greeks in Athens send human sacrifices to him. Eventually a Greek hero killed the Minotaur. Excavations on the palace this century have revealed murals  with young men and women using the horns of a bull to leap on to its back! Drinking vessels made in the shape of bulls' heads were also found and carvings of bulls' horns were even used to decorate the steps of the palace. Strange or what?!

A mural is a large painting on a wall. It comes from the Latin word for wall, *murus*.

## GLAMOUR AND GLITZ OF THE ANCIENT FUNERAL WORLD

Many ancient folk believed that when they died they were just entering another life and so would need everyday items from their current lives. Poor people might take pots and pans or a tiny piece of jade (the Ancient Chinese believed that jade would preserve the body after death) but rich people were often buried with numerous valuable items covered in decorations. Many of the ancient pieces of art we have today came from tombs.

### GRAVES AT UR

The ziggurat city of Ur (remember? see p13) had many rich rulers and their tombs lay outside the city. One of the kings was buried with over 70 servants - and they had probably been made to drink poison. Alongside the skeletons have been found various items. These include the remains of a harp-like instrument which

 BC means Before Christ, before the year 1 on our modern calendar. AD means from year 1 onwards. AD stands for the Latin *anno Domini* (in the year of our Lord).

was decorated with gold leaf and lapis lazuli, as well as beautiful headdresses made of gold, shaped like beech and willow leaves. The blue lapis lazuli stone was often used in works of art in these graves. It must have been very expensive because it was imported to Ur from over 2,000 miles away in northern Afghanistan.

PART OF
A HARP

## EGYPTIAN TOMBS

The richest treasures from Ancient Egypt were found in the tomb of an 18-year-old boy, the Pharaoh Tutankhamun. There were ornate tables, chairs, carriages, some jewellery - and even a fly swat! Tutankhamun's gold throne has a picture of himself and his wife on it, made out of semi-precious stones and coloured glass. His mummified face was covered by an amazing solid gold death mask. Yet the area of Tutankhamun's tomb was tiny compared to those of the other, older pharaohs - these tombs must have contained even more amazing goods before thieves stole them thousands of years ago!

## PAINTINGS AND DECORATIONS IN TOMBS

Ancient tombs were often decorated with wonderful pictures. In Egypt the painters wanted you to see the most important part of the object they were illustrating so, for example, they painted a person with the head and limbs shown from the side but the eyes and body from the front. Or a duck pond would be seen from above, but the ducks on it, fish in it and trees around it would be painted from a side view.

## GALLOPING GOODS

The Scythians, who galloped round eastern Europe and central Asia on horses 2,500 years ago, made all their items transportable so they could be easily carried when they packed up their tents and moved house. Their art was therefore always in a practical form - like a solid gold comb with lifelike carvings of people and horses. Any Scythian goods we have today were found in graves. The chiefs were also usually buried together with several horses, not to mention their wife and at least one servant. They planned a good life in the Afterworld!

---

### WARNING:

Watch what you put in your rubbish bin! The date of an ancient work of art can be worked out by measuring the deterioration of a form of carbon in nearby ancient rubbish dumps. You never know who might be rummaging through your rubbish in the future in the name of historical research!

---

 Many of the early cave paintings were painted this way too, and some art this century has sort of returned to this idea - see Cubism p107.

# GREEK GOODS AND ROMAN REMAINS

## CLASS STUFF!

### CLASSICAL ART

The art and architecture of the Ancient Greeks and Ancient Romans is known as *Classical Art*, meaning of the highest class, or best standard. The Greeks and Romans never actually called it that themselves, it was a term probably given to it from the 16th century when people in western Europe were copying it because they thought it was so wonderful.

## SO WHO COPIED WHO?

In fact throughout the ages the classical look seems to have been copied - even by the Greeks themselves. Although the Greeks are credited with starting it, they actually probably took others' ideas before them (some from the Ancient Egyptians) and developed these. Then, when the Romans came along, they copied and developed what the Greeks had done. For about 1,000 years no one then took much notice of the Classical style but for the last four hundred years or so it has had a great influence on European art and architecture again.

# GREEK GOODS

## BUILDINGS

The Ancient Greeks had lots of gods and temples were the most important buildings in Ancient Greece. These temples didn't *have* to be large as only the priests entered them, and they were meant to be a private place for that particular god - unlike Christian churches, where the worshippers should all be inside. In a Greek temple the altar was on the outside (on top of the temple, or on the front steps) and all festivities, sacrifices and so on, took place outside, where the crowds could see them. Temples were decorated in very bright colours and had statues in front of them. Inside was a statue of the particular god, or goddess.

## PILLARS AND COLUMNS

Early Greek temples were probably built in wood and then the style copied when they were later built in stone. Therefore the style of the pillars in the stone temples built by the Ancient Greeks seems to have developed from the wooden temples their ancestors had built which used tree trunks standing upright to support another piece of wood laid out along the top of them.

There are three main styles of stone Greek columns:

Doric - pretty simple, like a tree trunk.

Ionic - like a tree trunk with a curly bit on top. Some say this was based on the practice of decorating the tops of columns in former wooden temples with the horns of sacrificed lambs.

Corinthian - like a tree trunk with fancy twirly leafy things on top. It has been suggested that real leaves might have been stuck on top of the tree trunk pillars in ancient wooden temples.

## Optical Illusions

It's generally believed that classical architecture is straight and simple. However this is not entirely true!

Many of the apparently straight columns, and the slabs along the top and bottom, are actually *slightly curved* to make the whole structure look straight to the human eye. This is because parallel lines don't appear straight when seen from a distance.

Also the space between the columns in Greek buildings was *not exactly equal*. This was for reasons of optical illusion again - exactly spaced columns don't look equally spaced when seen from a distance!

## The Parthenon

The Parthenon is probably the most famous Greek building that still exists. It is made of marble, is in the Doric style, and it stands on top of a hill in the middle of Athens - the capital of both Ancient and modern Greece. It follows the Ancient Greek rules of architecture - it is 8 columns wide by 17 long (the rule was that the sides should have double the number of columns at the ends, plus one). It was built as a temple to the goddess Athena, the city's deity.

The famous Greek sculptor, Phidias (d. *c*. 432 BC), made a huge statue of the goddess Athena to put inside the Parthenon. The statue was 11 m high - as high as a tree - and made of gold, ivory and wood. Apparently at the main festival every year, she was given a new dress to put on! Like most Greek sculptures this statue of Athena is now lost - though there is a marble Roman copy, one metre high, in a museum in modern Athens.

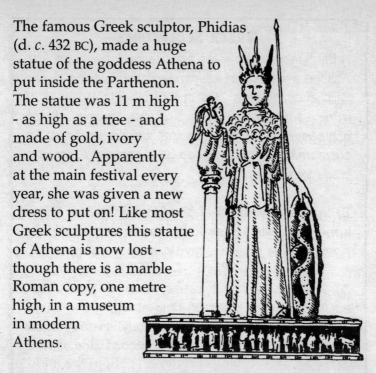

The Parthenon's history, since building started in 447 BC, has been varied. In the 5th century AD it was converted into a Christian church. When the Turks invaded Greece in the 15th century it became a mosque. Yet despite all this it remained virtually intact until the Venetians shelled it and blew out the centre because the Turks were using part of it as a store for gun powder. Nowadays what's left of the marble is disintegrating because of the pollution in modern Athens.

# GREEK SCULPTURES

1) Phidias was the most famous sculptor in ancient Athens and probably supervised the building of the Parthenon. However not one of his known pieces of work still survives! We are only aware of his achievements because ancient writers wrote about them and also because copies of some of them were made by the Romans.

2) In fact almost all of the famous Ancient Greek works of art that exist today are copies made by the Romans. The originals have long since disappeared.

3) That's a shame because we know that Greek sculptors spent a lot of time studying the shape and movement of the human body so they could make perfect figures of their gods and also of their athletes.

4) One of the very few original Greek statues that has survived is that of a bronze charioteer. It was found at Delphi, an ancient site north of Athens. He stands 180 cm high. He only has one arm now, but still manages to hold the reins of his horses.

5) If you were a Greek with a big head you might not have been too pleased with a statue of yourself as in many classical Greek statues the height of a person is shown as exactly eight times the length of the head.

# GREEK ART AND PAINTING

*Once upon a time...*

1) Art was often used to tell stories. Many Greek pots had pictures of the Greek hero Theseus battling with the Minotaur of Crete painted on to them (see p13). On pots and vases white paint was often used to represent female flesh, while red was sometimes male flesh.

2) Wall carvings and murals told stories too. A wall frieze 🦶 that survives from the *Mausoleum of Halicarnassus* (an enormous tomb which was built for ruler Mausolus by his wife - who was also his sister!) shows Greeks fighting with Amazons - and winning! The Greeks always seemed to be fighting someone!

3) Indeed, it seems from writings of the time that artists were actually more important than sculptors in Ancient Greece - shops and rich private houses often had paintings on the walls. However nowadays we are more aware of the sculptors' pieces of work than the painters' because some copies of sculptures have survived.

---

🦶 A *frieze* is a decorated strip on a wall.

4) Around 500 BC western painters stopped drawing all feet and hands as seen from the side like the Ancient Egyptians always had, but, when needed, started drawing them as if the viewer was looking at them from the front. In other words, people and objects began to be painted as the viewer saw them, with the front parts of the subject larger. This is called *foreshortening*.

5) About 300 BC profiles of Greek rulers began to appear on coins.

**STOP PRESS - STOP PRESS - STOP PRESS**

GREEK MYTHOLOGICAL TIMES

**Statue Brought to Life: Special report from Cyprus**

Lucky King Pygmalion of Cyprus has had his wishes granted and now has a beautiful woman in his life. But this is no ordinary lady. Until last week she was just a wonderful statue - albeit one that the king had fallen head over heels in love with. It is reported that the goddess of Love, Aphrodite, was listening in when he was talking to the silent beauty and answered the desperate man's prayers. Hopefully the former statue doesn't have too sharp a tongue!

DARLING, I LOVE YOU!

### Curtains for Zeuxis

Yesterday two of the most celebrated artists in the land had a competition. Both had reckoned that his painting was more realistic than the other's. Zeuxis first displayed some grapes that even fooled some birds into flying up to grab a quick bite. Looking rather smug Zeuxis walked over to pull back the curtain hanging in front of his rival Parrhasius' picture. The curtain was painted too.

# ROMAN REMAINS

## THE ETRUSCANS

I THOUGHT WE WERE GOING TO TALK ABOUT THE ROMANS!

YES, BUT THE ETRUSCANS CONTROLLED ROME TILL THE ROMANS CONQUERED THEM.

SO!

WELL, A LOT OF ROMAN ART AND ARCHITECTURE WAS INFLUENCED BY THEM.

EARLY ROMAN SCULPTURE

AS WELL AS BY THE GREEKS?

YES, THE ETRUSCANS IMPORTED AND COPIED LOTS OF GREEK THINGS LIKE THEIR VASES, STATUES AND PAINTINGS.

## DEATH MASKS

The early Romans (and the Estruscans before them) made wax death masks of their loved ones so they could remember them. They carried them in funeral processions and then they displayed them around the house in the same way that we might put out photographs. Later they would perhaps transfer these images into something more permanent like bronze or terracotta (baked clay).

The experience of making these wax death masks was probably why the later Romans were so good at making life-like busts  and portraits of emperors and other people. They were very good at doing the detailed features and structure of the human head. There was no flattering, even of an emperor - if he was ugly, his face on his bust looked ugly!

A bust is a sculpture of the head, upper shoulders and chest of a person.

## Copy ... Copy ... Copy ...Copy ... That's what the punter wants

As we've noted before, many of the Roman works of art were copies of Greek originals. But that's what the buyers wanted. And, as any salesman knows, "the customer is always right", and so the craftsmen made lots of money by producing endless copies. In fact many of the craftsmen and painters in Rome itself were actually Greeks.

## Awesome Arches

However, there was one thing the Romans did which the Greeks never really used in their buildings - the Romans built arches. They used arches to hold up aqueducts and bridges, and also to make roofs. They also made arches just for the sake of making arches! Some, called *triumphal arches*, were to celebrate great battles. These had reliefs (see p14) and words on them emphasising to passers-by how wonderful the Romans were. A few still stand today.

You have to make an arch out of separate wedge-shaped forms and it's pretty difficult to balance these to keep the arch standing up unless you really know what you are doing. The central stone, or *key-stone*, is the most important.

## THE COLOSSEUM

The Colosseum in Rome is probably the most famous Roman building that remains today - although it is pretty ruined. (In Latin the word *colosseus* means enormous, gigantic - and colossal!). There was room for 50,000 people inside this arena! The spectators watched Christians being thrown to lions and gladiators battling with each other here. There were three layers of arches to support the seats inside. The architect also incorporated the three styles of column used by the Greeks for building temples - Doric, Ionic, and Corinthian. Roman writings tell us that when the

Colosseum was opened, in about AD 80, it was flooded with water so that the celebrations could include a mock sea-battle with 3,000 "sailors"!

## THE PANTHEON

The Pantheon, a temple dedicated to *all* the Roman gods, was also built in Rome and, amazingly, still remains intact today. It has survived for two thousand years. The reason that the Pantheon has lasted all this time is that, although it was originally built as a Roman temple, it became a Christian church in AD 609 and has been one ever since. Therefore the people of Rome have always looked after this building because it has always played a very important part in their religious life.

The Romans used the techniques from their arch building to build an enormous dome on top of the Pantheon. The very centre of the dome has a large circular opening (9 m in diameter) which lets the light in - in fact this is the only source of light in the building. This opening also lets the rain in! Directly underneath, in the centre of the floor, the Romans made a drain to let this water out.

---

## WHAT A RELIEF!

The Romans were into relief carvings in a big way. They did lots and lots between about 100 BC and AD 400 on walls, arches and columns. They were often of great Roman military victories - hey, just like the Greeks and Assyrians! It was all a form of propaganda to say how fantastic they were.

---

### STATUES

*Mistaken Identity*

A more than life-size bronze statue of the Roman Emperor Marcus Aurelius on a horse has only survived to today, from the second century, because people in the Middle Ages thought it was of the first Christian Roman Emperor, Constantine, rather than of a pagan (un-Christian) ruler. Otherwise it would have been melted down, like every other pagan statue in the very

Christian Middle Ages in Europe when metal was badly needed.

In fact a copy now stands in the statue's original place in Rome and the statue itself is in a museum because of the threat of pollution.

## POMPEII PAINTINGS

The best examples that exist of Roman painting are those inside villas, houses and shops in Pompeii, a small town in what is now southern Italy. Pompeii was completely covered by ash when the nearby volcano of Vesuvius erupted in AD 79. Pompeii was excavated in the mid 19th century and wonderful wall paintings and mosaics were found. These paintings were of a whole range of subjects: still lifes, such as fruit and flowers, countryside scenes, theatrical scenes and, of course, people. Pompeii was just a small town, so what would the paintings have been like in the larger cities? We can only guess. The excavators also discovered spaces in the ash where people had suffocated as they were buried. The archeologists in 1864 injected liquid plaster into these spaces to make plastercasts of the bodies - if that was done nowadays this itself would probably be regarded as a new kind of art!

## MAKING MOSAICS

Rich Romans often decorated the floors of their houses with mosaics. Mosaics are decorations on floors and walls made of small squarish coloured stones, coloured bits of glass, pieces of painted baked clay and similar materials. The stones were usually found in the local countryside - so the stones and materials used in mosaics in Romans' houses in far flung parts of the Roman Empire (like modern England or Spain) would have been different from those used in Pompeii. The Romans made mosaic pictures of plants and animals, portrayed scenes from stories and legends, or just created abstract patterns.

The Romans weren't the first, or last, to use mosaics to decorate - we know that the Ancient Sumerians (see p13) members of the Byzantine Empire (see p37) and the Aztecs (AD 1100-1521) decorated their buildings with mosaics.

31

# MEANWHILE, ELSEWHERE IN THE WORLD ...

While the Ancient Egyptians, Greeks and Romans were busily building, painting and decorating, people in the rest of the world were being creative too.

## CHINESE 'DINGS'

In China three and a half thousand years ago craftsmen made bronze vessels decorated with grinning human faces and amazing animals. These were used for preparing and serving food and wine, and for ceremonies and sacrifices. One of the most common type seems to have been the *ding* - a three or four legged vessel which could be anything from 15 cm to 120 cm in size. The Chinese did - and still do - worship their ancestors, and these dings were for presenting food and wine to them. Sculptures and jewellery have also been found from this time in China.

## CHINESE TOMB

In China, about 2,200 years ago, the first Chinese Emperor, Qin Shi Huang Di, had 7,000 terracotta soldiers made to guard his grave. All the faces are different and they are probably copied from the real members of the Emperor's army. Some show the features of people from races on the very edge of Qin Shi Huang Di's empire. Little bits of colour show that their clothes were once painted bright yellows, purples and greens!

## A Chinese Wall

The same Emperor, Qin Shi Huang Di, started building The Great Wall of China to keep out the enemies he feared might invade his territory. The remains of The Wall now stretch over 3,000 km across northern China. It can even be seen from the Moon!

## Nok Nok

In what is now Nigeria in West Africa, in about 500 BC, the Nok people produced life-like terracotta figures of animals - monkeys, elephants and snakes - and human beings. Each human figure seems to have a particular personality of its own shown by different facial expressions. Many of the heads are life-size but attached to smaller bodies. The faces are probably portraits of Nok ancestors, made out of terracotta so they, and the magic in them, would survive. The type of carving (with sharp, deep cuts into the terracotta) indicates that the Nok people first carved in wood. Sadly the Nok people seem to have vanished about AD 300, but they did have a great influence on the art of West Africa for centuries to come - so the magic of the ancestors obviously worked!

## THE HEADS OF THE OLMECS

The Olmecs lived in what is now Mexico for roughly 1,000 years from about 1300-400 BC. They carved enormous stone heads - of their gods or leaders perhaps? One which still exists today is 180 cm high, is wearing a helmet and has earrings! Some of the Olmecs' other types of sculptures survive. These include small jade figures of infants with growling jaguars' snouts!

## WOVEN PERUVIAN SHAWLS

In Peru over 2,000 years ago garments woven with decorated figures were wrapped round the bodies of the dead in graves. Many of these have survived today because of the very dry soil on the coast there. It is quite likely that the upper classes wore these fancy shawls in the normal way and that they were buried with them so that they could look smart in the next life.

## PERSIAN CARPETS

The oldest Persian carpet in the world, 2,500 years old, was found this century in a Scythian tomb (see p16) in the Altai Mountains in Central Asia. Water had seeped into the tomb not long after it had been closed and then frozen. Everything was then encased in solid ice for centuries and so preserved.

---

*Olmecs* means "dwellers in the land of rubber".

# EUROPEAN ART IN THE MIDDLE AGES

In the Middles Ages (*c.* AD 500-1500) in Europe the Christian religion spread and grew in popularity and had an enormous influence on all types of art.

## "SSSSHHHHHH! DON'T TELL ANYONE WHAT WE'RE UP TO!"

Christians believe that Jesus Christ was born in part of the Roman Empire. Later a Roman Governor, Pontius Pilot, ordered his death. The Roman state wasn't too keen on Christians because they said there should be only one God, rather than the hundreds that the Romans worshipped in their various temples.

So, as the Christian belief seemed to be threatening the very fabric of the Roman Empire, Christians were thrown to lions in the Colosseum and other arenas. In light of this, to admit to being a Christian was not a good idea. Therefore, although Christianity developed during the last couple of hundred years of the Roman Empire, the first Christians had to worship in secret.

In Rome itself the Christians often met in underground burial places called *catacombs* which were a system of tunnels under the city with niches for the tombs. Pictures of people from Bible stories have been found on the walls of catacombs. The Christians also had secret symbols they used in pictures which only other Christians would recognise - like a fish (the first letters of the Greek words for "Jesus Christ, God's Son, Saviour" spell "fish" in Greek!).

ICHTHYS
=FISH

## A NEW MAN

But everything changed when the Roman Emperor Constantine converted to Christianity in AD 311 and made it the state religion. It was now perfectly all right to be a Christian. LARGE CHURCHES were built because, unlike with a temple which could be quite small as processions and sacrifices took place outside, all the worshippers had to be inside the church at the same time.

But people were not allowed to put statues in these because this was like having images of gods in the old temples. The Church thought ordinary folk would think that they were worshipping the statue rather than God.

Many Christians were also pretty *against* paintings.

*Then the old Roman Empire split into two parts:*

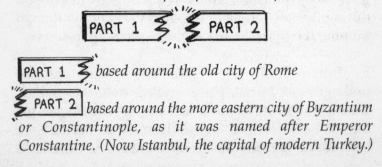

PART 1 ⋛ ⋛ PART 2

PART 1 ⋛ *based around the old city of Rome*

⋛ PART 2 *based around the more eastern city of Byzantium or Constantinople, as it was named after Emperor Constantine. (Now Istanbul, the capital of modern Turkey.)*

## PART 1

**Early Western European Christianity and Painting**

Luckily for the history of painting, at the end of the sixth century Pope Gregory the Great said that religious paintings should be allowed in churches and elsewhere as they would be useful to teach the Bible stories to people who could not read or write. But, from their very beginnings, Christians had never been really interested in painting pictures of *real* people or scenes because the artists were more concerned about getting a message across than doing a representative painting. It was almost like going back to the Egyptian idea of putting the most important things into the painting and not worrying about the rest. Many of the figures in Christian art at this time were pretty stiff and unreal looking. But it did become usual after Pope Gregory's announcement to have religious pictures in churches.

## PART 2

**Early Eastern European Christianity and Painting**
(also called *Byzantine Art* - after the old name for Constantinople)

In the eastern part of the old Roman Empire, where people didn't follow what the western Pope said, ardent Christians stated that there should be no religious images *at all, anywhere*. And there weren't for about a hundred years from AD 754.

Then another group gained influence and said, "Yes, you can have pictures but they must be the same as the ones before". They reckoned that not any old painting could be used as a "true sacred image" or religious "icon"  , but only the traditional types. These were of Christ and his mother, the Virgin Mary. The strict formal rules were stuck to again and again. However the very fact the artists did stick to these very strict rules did mean that some of the Greek ideas for depicting clothes, faces and gestures were kept going.

## HEY, DON'T FORGET US!

From the 5th century AD the Roman Empire in the West came under the influence of people like the Goths, the Anglo-Saxons and, later, the Vikings, who had other gods and types of art. These people were very good at working with metal and at carving wood. Excavation of the grave of an Anglo-Saxon warrior chief in England revealed, among other things, an amazing bronze helmet decorated with strange creatures and a gold buckle designed with a pattern of continuous swirls and squirls. Viking prows on the front of their battle ships were carved in terrifying

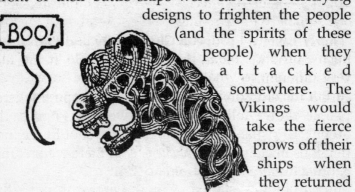

designs to frighten the people (and the spirits of these people) when they attacked somewhere. The Vikings would take the fierce prows off their ships when they returned

---

In the Christian religion an *icon* is an image or symbol of a saint or other holy person, sometimes regarded as sacred in itself and holding special powers. It comes from a Greek word *eikon* meaning "likeness".

home, so the spirits in their own lands would not be frightened!

## DRAGONS IN MONASTERIES

Between about the 5th and 10th centuries in western Europe the only Christian art that really happened was in monasteries and convents. There was quite a lot of confusion, war and turmoil in the rest of the place at this time. These Christian artists were actually influenced by the art of the other non-Christian people hanging around, like the early Anglo-Saxons, and, in Ireland, the early Celts. Celtic art too was full of complicated patterns. These often included intertwined bodies of dragons, birds and other animals - some mythical. The monks, who were writing out the gospels and other Christian and historical texts in Latin often used these sort of designs in the decoration of their pages. Sometimes these brightly-coloured patterns were very complicated and one square centimetre might take several days for the artist to do by hand! The Book of Kells, written in Ireland around AD 800, is done in this style. It was all very different to what was happening in the eastern part of the old Roman Empire with icons and things!

## A NEW TYPE OF ARCHITECTURE

*A different approach to art (well, a bit!)*

Church building started again in earnest in the 11th century in western Europe. There were less wars and so people felt inspired to build. These new buildings gave more opportunities for other types of art to be displayed inside. Many of the churches in the 11th and

12th centuries were built with rounded arches (in the 19th century this style was given the name *Romanesque* because it was influenced by the Roman arches). Carvings and paintings in these new buildings told Bible stories.

In the 13th and 14th centuries enormous cathedrals began to be built . Some took over a hundred years to be completed. Cologne Cathedral, in Germany, was started in 1248 and not completed until 1880! These cathedrals built (or begun!) in the 13th and 14th centuries have pointed arches and spires which their builders believed pointed towards heaven. In the 17th century this style was given the name *Gothic*, because it was believed to have been inspired by barbarians, the Goths. Gothic was meant to be a term of abuse. However in the 19th century in Europe this style was back in fashion again - both with people, and with vampires!

 Many of these cathedrals were decorated with statues and sculptures which were sometimes painted in bright colours.

40

## Stained Glass Windows

Lots of Gothic cathedrals and churches had stained glass windows. They were made from coloured glass joined together with lead. The daylight behind them lit up the religious scenes on them. It was a bit like having colour television in the church!

## Tapestries and Embroideries

Enormous tapestries and embroideries were used to decorate (and warm) the walls in castles, cathedrals and churches. In churches and cathedrals they would have religious scenes on them. Sometimes a series of them told a story around a room. The most famous "tapestry" of all from this time, the Bayeux Tapestry, is in fact not a tapestry at all but an embroidery on linen! It tells the story of the invasion of England by the Normans in 1066. There are lots of soldiers, horses and arrows on it - and lots of death scenes!

## Portraits

Well, actually there weren't many in the 11th century! At least, not of individual people looking like individual people. Artists mostly just drew a Middle Ages-looking figure and if he was a king put a crown on his head and a sceptre in his hand. A bishop would have a bishop's hat and crook. Then the name of the individual it was meant to represent was written underneath.

# MEDIEVAL ART SCHOOLS

If you wanted to be an artist in the Middle Ages you joined a successful artist's workshop as an apprentice/student and first got taught how to mix paints for the boss. Then you learnt how to copy the traditional styles and approaches. Never would you have to draw something from real life! Artists were regarded as craftsmen and belonged to guilds. 🦶

# MEDIEVAL COLOURS

The two most important colours in medieval times were blue and gold - really because they were so expensive. The amount of blue and gold to be used was always put into a contract! Blue came from crushed lapis lazuli (see p15), which had to be imported from the East, while the gold was real gold leaf, hammered and hammered and hammered as thin as possible, in fact until you could see through it! Blue was used for the clothes of the most important people in the picture (like the Virgin Mary's gown) and gold was used for halos 🦶 and decorations. As much gold as possible was always used because it reflected the light of the candles in the dark churches.

---

A *guild* was an association of people working in the same craft area, eg artists, carpenters.

*Halos* were painted flat until about 1450.

## MEDIEVAL SCENES

These are mostly Bible stories. Usually the main action is in the foreground and earlier incidents are in the background - for example the three kings with baby Jesus in the foreground and in the background them setting out on their journey. The *size* of the figures and objects reflects their importance, not what the distance between them in the picture is. The French *Book of Hours* by the Limburg Brothers is an illustrated prayer book from the 15th century which does have some scenes of everyday life in it such as ploughing. It is also an early example in the medieval period of the artist painting in shadows (such as of the horse pulling the plough etc). This is a very exciting development, nearly as exciting as Giotto ...

## GIOTTO

*An Artist with a Name - albeit a bit of a Shady Character!*
In the early 14th century an Italian artist called Giotto di Bondone (c.1267-1337), from the city of Florence, got a bit bored with the flat unrealistic paintings everyone had been doing for so long and tried out some new approaches when he was painting the walls of the tiny Arena chapel in Padua, northern Italy, with scenes from Christ's life. Rather than just adapting older representations of these scenes and producing stiff unreal looking figures (as had been the custom for ages and ages and ages now), Giotto used shading and the old trick of foreshortening (see p24) to create depth on a flat surface. He also tried to show people's feelings in their faces. It was revolutionary! No one

had used these techniques for a thousand years and everyone thought Giotto was wonderful. In fact he became a household name in Italy. The status of the artist had begun to change.

## FRESCOS

*Fresco* means "fresh" in Italian. The famous paintings Giotto did on the walls of the church in Padua were frescos - they were painted on the walls when the plaster was still fresh or wet. Pretty difficult. If the artist gets the technique the scene will last for hundreds of years as when the paint dries it is part of the wall and can't flake off. That's why frescos were used to paint bible stories on the walls of churches. However if the plaster is too wet the paint drips or if the plaster is too dry the paint cracks. Sometimes it can just go mouldy. Giotto was obviously a bit of a whizzkid at frescos.

## CARTOONS

No, not the "ha, ha, ha" type of picture! These were full-sized designs for pictures, often kept as final pictures in themselves, which artists from the time of Giotto (apart from Giotto because he was so confident in his skills!) used. One way of transferring the design on to the final surface was to make pin-prick holes around the drawing and then rub powdered charcoal through them. This gave an outline for the painting. The modern use of the word *cartoon* comes from the 19th century when some designs for frescos in the English House of Commons were made fun of in a magazine with - yes, you've got it! - funny drawings!!

# AWAY FROM THE WEST

## PATTERNS, NOT PEOPLE
## - THE MIDDLE EAST

While Christianity was sweeping through Europe, the Islamic religion took hold in the Middle East. This religion was founded in the early 600s by the prophet Mohammed. For the people who practise this religion, the Muslims, the making of images is totally and utterly forbidden. No figures of people or animals should appear in any piece of artwork at all. Therefore the craftsmen in the Islamic areas began to create more and more wonderful patterns to decorate their buildings and rugs. Writing was also very important as part of the design.

Later on, some Muslims were less strict about this. In Persia figures could be painted as long as the scenes they were shown in had nothing to do with religion. In the 14th century wonderful brightly coloured pictures were done in Persia of ancient stories from the area. These were often tiny miniature illustrations for books with lots and lots of detail in them. In these pictures the things that are happening in the foreground are at the bottom of the picture. The things happening behind them are above them in the picture - and so on in sort of "strips". So although characters and flowers at the top and bottom of the picture are of the same size the ones at the top are actually in the distance. It's a system the viewers understood and in these pictures everything looks balanced as if in a pattern.

## INDIAN ART

In India religion had a strong influence on art too.

HINDU SCULPTURES
The main religion in India, Hinduism, influenced sculptures of the various Hindu gods. These figures seemed to be full of emotion and feeling, very different to the static sculptures in Europe in the Middle Ages.

BUDDHIST STATUES Buddhism started about 600 BC in India. The Buddhist art was influenced by the Hindu style but some statues and reliefs of the Buddha (the young prince who founded Buddhism) from about AD 200 in the western part of India show evidence of influences from Greece.

OTHER INFLUENCES ON INDIAN ART...

When India was invaded by Muslim warriors from the Middle East in the 16th century these newcomers, the Moguls, set up an empire in the North of India. The Moguls had been influenced by Persian and Chinese art and brought with them the style of painting tiny pictures. As in Persia these paintings were brightly coloured and very detailed. The Mogul rulers didn't really want religious scenes and the pictures they commissioned often show scenes of their families in their rich palaces and wonderful gardens. Some fantastic illustrated books from this time still exist.

Hindus also started to paint their religious pictures in this new style. In these types of Hindu paintings the Hindu god, Krisha, was usually painted with blue skin.

... AND ON INDIAN ARCHITECTURE

It was a Mogul Emperor who built the Taj Mahal, the most famous building in India - perhaps in the world. This beautiful large white building is really an enormous tomb. The Emperor made it for his wife when she died - what a way to be remembered! It is said that the Emperor intended to build an exact copy of this building, but in black, on the other side of the river as a tomb for himself. He fell on hard times, however, after building her one and is in fact buried beside her in it. His sepulchre is the only thing that is not symmetrical in the whole of the Taj Mahal complex. No figures appear in the decorations of the Taj, just amazing patterns and flowers.

## CHINESE CHARACTERISTICS

China too was a happening place at this time. Between AD 618 and 907 the Tang dynasty was ruling China. Their leaders were really into the arts.

PAINTING

Landscape painting became the "in" thing. What the artist had to do was go and sit for hours, days perhaps, looking at a landscape and thinking about it. Then, when he felt he was ready he had to rush inside and paint it very quickly; no changes were allowed once he'd got going! These artists would have spent many years practising doing this and studying the works of previous Chinese artists.

Yes, the paintings do all look more or less the same - a hazy mountain in the background, some trees in the foreground, a river or a gorge and perhaps a few small people - but that was the way to do it in China. Stillness and simplicity were the aim of these pictures. The Chinese expression for "landscape painting" literally means "mountains and water". In fact Chinese painting techniques changed little for hundreds of years after that.

These pictures were placed on silk scrolls which were then rolled open and studied in the same way we might read a bit of a book that we really like. Some of these scrolls were 30 metres long and were looked at section by section as they were unrolled, rather than all 30 metres together!

The Chinese also painted animals and people. A lot of Chinese pictures have symbolic meanings - for example a fish is the symbol of prosperity and fertility.

## WRITING

Writing was also an art form in China - and still is. The art of handwriting is called *calligraphy*, and the Chinese hung their calligraphy on their walls like pictures. But not just anybody could do this; a calligrapher had to have years of training in how to hold the brush and the techniques needed. (The Chinese hold their brushes in a different way to Westerners.)

## STATUES & SCULPTURES

Chinese sculptures were often pretty curvy. A prancing horse, for example, was often made in a rounded way. Evidence in tombs also shows that religion had a great influence on art in China too. And Chinese art influenced Japanese and other Asian art.

## ART ELSEWHERE

EASTER ISLAND STATUES

Over 600 enormous statues
- of heads and of heads
with the upper body -
stand on Easter Island in
the Pacific Ocean. Some are
as high as 18.3 m. They are
made from volcanic rock
and all face the sea. They
were set up between AD 400
and 1600 by the
Polynesians. Easter
Island is a very long way
away from anywhere -
1,250 miles from the
nearest island.

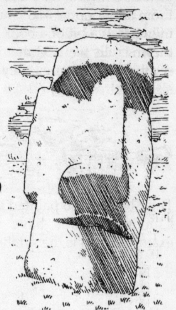

BENIN BRONZES

In the 12th century the people in Benin in West Africa
(modern Nigeria) were commissioning wonderful
bronze heads of their ancestors from nearby Ife. They
then started making them themselves. They also made
bronze plaques showing scenes from their histories
and their ways of life. But everything had to be
ordered by the king. If a bronze-caster made
something the king had not authorised, the
punishment was death! Bronze-casting
continued here till the late 19th century
when the British arrived and put a stop
to all aspects of the traditional Benin
way of life (including making sacrifices
to the "devil" in times of stress).

## MAYAN CARVINGS

From about AD 100-1000 the Mayan people, who lived in what is now Central America, made wonderful carvings on the buildings they built, carvings of the death-god (who looked a bit like a skull) and other things.

## THE NAZCA LINES

For nearly 1000 years, between about 500 BC and AD 700, in the stony desert of what is now modern Peru, the Nazca Lines were created by the Nazca people (200 BC - AD 600) and others. These people (we think!) cleared millions of small stones covering the sand to make long straight lines and enormous diagrams of plants, animals and birds - one bird has a wing-span of over 100 metres. There is even a spider over *46 m* long - horrible!! Some people have suggested that these were not actually made by human beings but by invaders from outer space... There are also shapes like triangles made in the desert - perhaps the landing strips of ancient astronauts ...?

# THE RENAISSANCE

## WHAT? WHY? HOW?

### THE EARLY RENAISSANCE IN 15TH CENTURY ITALY

The 15th century was a time of questioning, learning and discovery by artists, sculptors, architects, writers, scientists and others in Italy and elsewhere in Europe. Everyone wanted to know What? Why? How?

### THE EIGHT ARTISTIC PS OF THE EARLY RENAISSANCE

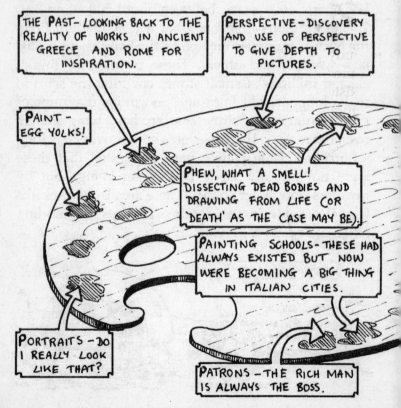

THE PAST- LOOKING BACK TO THE REALITY OF WORKS IN ANCIENT GREECE AND ROME FOR INSPIRATION.

PERSPECTIVE - DISCOVERY AND USE OF PERSPECTIVE TO GIVE DEPTH TO PICTURES.

PAINT - EGG YOLKS!

PHEW, WHAT A SMELL! DISSECTING DEAD BODIES AND DRAWING FROM LIFE (OR 'DEATH' AS THE CASE MAY BE).

PAINTING SCHOOLS- THESE HAD ALWAYS EXISTED BUT NOW WERE BECOMING A BIG THING IN ITALIAN CITIES.

PORTRAITS - DO I REALLY LOOK LIKE THAT?

PATRONS - THE RICH MAN IS ALWAYS THE BOSS.

# THE PAST

In 15th century Italy more and more artists, like Giotto before them, began to get a bit bored with painting in the same way all the time. They started to ask questions and try out new techniques. They, along with sculptors and architects, started to look back to the realistic work of Ancient Greece and Rome for inspiration. In their search for knowledge they were looking back to move forward. This is why the time became known as the *Renaissance*, which means "rebirth" or "revival" (in French actually, but don't let that confuse you!)

*Problems for 15th century painters looking to the past*
However it was easier for sculptors and architects to study the styles of the classical period than artists. Ruins of buildings and some sculptured figures still existed, but there were only a few fragments of murals. The Pompeii pictures were not discovered until 300 years later (see p83). Painters had to rely on classical literature and the stories like Zeuxis and Parrhasius' competition (see p25). They wanted to paint pictures as real as this.

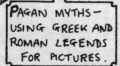

PAGAN MYTHS — USING GREEK AND ROMAN LEGENDS FOR PICTURES.

# ERSPECTIVE

But not all the answers at this time came from the Ancient World. A new way of working out how to show things in the distance in a picture was calculated in Florence in the 15th century. *Perspective* is the word used to describe this technique. Not only were things in the distance made smaller (as had been done before) but a grid was used to work out exactly what size they should be and where they should be placed in relation to the images in the foreground of the picture. These imaginary lines all lead to a vanishing point in the distance. In the picture below you can see the vanishing point of the left-hand side of the temple. The trick was to paint the images as if you were standing in a particular spot. If you moved one step forward or back the vanishing point would be different. The use of these new rules gave depth to the pictures and made items, especially people, look more solid and real. On frescos in some Italian churches the use of perspective makes it look as though the people in the pictures are actually about to get up and join the people in the church!

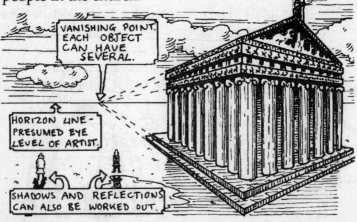

# PHEW, WHAT A SMELL!

In Florence and elsewhere in Italy artists began to study the human body and how it worked. Some were so interested in getting the people in their pictures right that they cut up dead bodies to look at them more closely - although this was illegal and the penalties were harsh. But still painters stole bodies and cut them up in secret. All in the name of Art!

# PAGAN MYTHS

In the late 15th century artists in Florence like Botticelli (1445-1510), began to use stories and characters from Ancient Greek and Roman myths and legends. Hey, pagan gods! It was quite a step to move away from Christian religious paintings. Some painters actually gave them a Christian interpretation - what would the early Christians have thought?!

Botticelli is not this guy's real name (he was really called Alessandro di Mariano Filipepi). *Botticelli* actually means "little barrel". This nickname was first given to his elder brother because he was bit fat, but then the rest of the family seem to have decided to use it as a surname!

One of Botticelli's most famous pictures is *The Birth of Venus*. The model was called Simonetta Vespucci. The continent of America is actually named after her cousin - a navigator and explorer called Amerigo Vespucci!

# PORTRAITS

These began to be very popular in Florence and elsewhere in Europe. Italian artists copied the style of portraits on Roman coins and medals. These

showed only the head and shoulders from the side view, or *profile*. It was difficult to flatter the sitter from this angle so it was reckoned to be the truest representation of someone. It was terrible if you had a big nose! Later in the 15th century Italian artists used to paint people in three-quarters profile, often with a landscape as a background.

# PAINTING SCHOOLS

Nearly all of the famous Renaissance artists learnt their skills in the painting school/studio of a successful artist.

# PATRONS

Artists at this time did not just paint a picture of something that had inspired them and then hope to sell it. Churches, town councils, rich merchants and members of the nobility would *commission* a special piece of work from a particular

I WANT TO BE THE BIGGEST PERSON IN THE PICTURE!

artist. The artist would go to discuss this with the patron to find out exactly what was wanted and where it would be placed. Contracts would be drawn up stating the price, size and subject matter. The contract might also state the number of figures in a picture and the colours to be used. Usually the artist had his own workshop and so, after planning the painting, a lot of the work was done by assistants. The more the patron paid, the more work the artist himself did. Sometimes the patron and his family would be painted into the crowd scenes of a religious picture. In Florence a powerful and rich family of merchants and bankers called the *Medici* commissioned many works of art in the 15th and 16th centuries. This sort of patronage gave artists a much higher social status than before. Some, such as Botticelli, became quite important and influential.

## PAINT

*Egg paint:* In 15th century Italy artists made their own paints. They mixed egg yolk with water and pigment made from ground down colours (taken from berries or metals). This type of "egg" painting was called *tempera.* They then painted the picture on to a wooden panel.

HE MUST BE WORKING ON A BIG PAINTING!

## EARLY RENAISSANCE PEOPLE:

(Notice they are all from Florence - it was the "arty place" to be at this time!)

*The Florentine painter Daddi (d.1348)* "signed" his work with a dice. *Daddi* means "dice" in Italian.

*The Florentine sculptor Donatello (c.1386-1466)* was the greatest European sculptor of the 15th century. He made an amazing bronze statue of David (the boy who killed the giant Goliath in the Bible) - the most lifelike statue anyone had made since Roman and Greek times. The work of Donatello had a great influence on Michelangelo.

*The Florentine architect Brunelleschi (1377-1447)* gave up sculpture and became an architect after he lost an important sculpture competition to design doors for the cathedral in Florence. He ending up designing the dome for the cathedral!

# The Renaissance in Northern Europe

There were a lot of very keen artists in northern Europe too at this time - and a lot of rich merchants to fund them. In the Netherlands and Flanders (now Belgium) many people had made money in the wool trade and could commission pictures and portraits. Painters here too were keen to make things look real.

## Jan van Eyck (1390-1441)

One bright Flemish painter, Jan van Eyck, is said to have invented oil paint - oh, and his brother Hubert is given some credit too! They mixed paint pigment with oil (instead of egg yolk and water like the Italians) and - voilà! - the paint dried much more slowly. This meant you didn't have to worry so much about making mistakes because you could change your painting quite easily before it dried  . As it was also now possible to paint more slowly you could paint in much more detail. It was also easier to be realistic. People said the flowers Jan van Eyck painted looked so real you could definitely smell them! The oil paint produced rich, jewel-like colours.

NOT MOTOR OIL, ANDY!

## Bosch (c.1450-1516)

Another Flemish painter of this time was Hieronymus Bosch. This guy painted weird and wonderful scenes full of monsters and ugly creatures - like people with fish heads and scissor legs! The Church condemned

---

 In some paintings the oil has become transparent with age and it is possible to see the corrected mistakes!

him and people avoided him. But boy, did he have an imagination - he would definitely be in demand as a sci-fi film maker now! The funny thing is he never left his home town, Hertogenbosch, which he was named after. His real name was Jerome van Aken.

## Dürer (1471-1528)

A German artist, Albrecht Dürer, travelled to Italy to get some ideas at this time (he should have gone north to see Mr Bosch instead, the whole cult of sci-fi might have started much earlier then!). He used the new technique of printing to spread the ideas like perspective he found in Italy. He engraved, or cut, a picture on to a block of wood or a piece of metal; this was then covered with ink, pressed down on to paper and, hey presto!, he had his print (yep, that's right, it *is* a bit like potato cuts). Prints became very popular because they were cheaper than paintings.

Poor Dürer. He was so inquisitive he wanted to find out about everything. Once he heard about a whale stranded on a beach and rushed to see it. However on this expedition he caught a fever which made him unwell for the rest of his life.

## Hans Holbein (1497/8-1543)

Although Hans was German he spent a lot of time in England at Henry VIII's court painting portraits of various important people. These portraits looked more like the people than the ones painted by many artists before (in the Middle Ages see p41). Except for one ... When King Henry was looking for yet another wife, Holbein was sent to Germany to paint a picture of Anne of Cleves, as dating agencies in those days couldn't provide photographs. When Henry saw the portrait he thought Anne of Cleves was so pretty he decided to marry her. He wasn't as pleased with her looks when she arrived and almost immediately divorced the poor lady. Hans was probably lucky to keep his head!

## SKULLS AND OTHER THINGS ...

One of Holbein's most famous paintings *The Ambassadors* has a squashed skull below the feet of the two dignified gentlemen he is painting. It's meant to symbolise that everyone dies. Symbols such as these were very important in paintings at this time.

## PIETER BRUEGEL (c.525-1569)

Another Flemish painter. He did pictures of everyday life - quite a change from a lot of other people's pictures. One, called *Children's Games* has an enormous number of children playing different games in it. Find a copy of it (have a look in the back of the book for suggestions where to go), and look for tug-of-war and leapfrog.

TUG OF WAR

# THE HIGH RENAISSANCE

Clever clogs call the years from 1500 to 1527 in Italy the *High Renaissance* as they think this was when some of the greatest achievements in art were made, especially in the use of colour and light - in just 27 years in the history of the world!

Florence had been the "in" city for quite a long time but now Rome was the place to hang out if you were an artist. No doubt that was something to do with the fact that the popes were ordering lots of pieces of artwork!

Three artists were hailed above all the others at this time:

LEONARDO DA VINCI 1452-1519
RAPHAEL 1483-1520
MICHELANGELO 1475-1564

## LEONARDO DA VINCI

Leonardo da Vinci has often been called the "Renaissance Man" because he was into everything. He had his fingers in a lot of pies. As well as painting he sculpted, and was also an architect, musician and military engineer. He drew plans for aeroplanes, helicopters and submarines! He also solved drainage problems in France when he was working at the court of the French king. (He was supposed to be very good looking too!)

When Leonardo was young he joined the workshop of a painter called Verrocchio. Apparently Verrocchio thought his new student was such a genius that he threw away his own paint brushes and never painted again!

Leonardo's most famous painting is the *Mona Lisa* - the most famous (and most valuable) painting in the world. The sitter is probably Lisa Gherardini, the wife of a Florentine banker. She has a smirk on her face and it is difficult to tell what she is thinking. Apparently Leonardo hired some musicians to entertain her while he was painting. Leonardo used soft colours which create a hazy mysterious effect. People say she sometimes looks sad and sometimes happy. Like a living person, they say, her expression seems to change. The painting of her was once larger but is has been chopped a bit. There used to be columns on the edge of the picture - in fact you can still see the bottom of one at the side of the painting. Her eyes are said to follow you.

Apparently the banker didn't like the picture of his wife and refused to pay for it. Later Leonardo sold it to Francis I the King of France who is said to have hung it in his bathroom for a while. That's why it's now in the Louvre Museum in Paris. Yet, believe it or not, it has been said that this picture of the Mona Lisa in the Louvre might not be genuine. The original was stolen from the museum in 1912 and during its three year disappearance six fakes turned up, each one selling for a lot of money.

Leonardo kept hundreds of notebooks of sketches and wrote endless notes ... in mirror writing! So how do you write in mirror writing? He was probably left-handed and found it easier to write his notes from right to left. Like many of his contemporaries, he was into cutting up dead bodies to study the human form, and made lots of sketches of these too - even of unborn babies. His work books show that he dissected over thirty corpses. He only stopped doing this when the Pope insisted.

THAT'S ENOUGH, LEONARDO!

He didn't believe anything he read and wanted to study everything. That was why he had so many notebooks, because he recorded everything in them. He based his aeroplane designs on how birds and insects fly.

Leonardo was so busy researching and questioning that he never seemed to get time to finish his paintings and other pieces. Many of his projects were never completed, like a bronze statue of a horse rearing up for the Duke of Milan.

# MICHELANGELO BUONARROTI (1475-1564)

One of the most famous, and greatest, artists ever was always known by his first name - Michelangelo. Ask someone who thinks they know all about art, "Who was signor Buonarroti?". They will probably have no idea!

Michelangelo was excellent at architecture, painting and poetry but he got his biggest kicks from making statues of people. He used to joke that the reason he liked working with stone so much was because, when he was very young, he was sent to live with a family of stonecutters because his mother couldn't look after him.

Michelangelo's father didn't want him to be an artist because in those days it was regarded as a lowly type of job. However, at the age of 13, he persuaded his father to let him became an apprentice at the workshop of a popular Florentine painter. One of the things he probably learnt there was how to paint a fresco (see p44). Learning about fresco painting certainly paid off because this "sculptor's" greatest work of art was to be a ceiling painted with frescos. Also the status of an artist was to change during his lifetime. Some, like himself, became important influential people.

But before this bit of decorating Michelangelo did get to do some sculpting. At the age of 23 in Rome he created a *Pietà* (statue of the dead Christ lying on his mother's knee) for a Cardinal in Rome. This was so successful that the people in his home town of Florence then gave him a huge block of marble as a gift. They wanted him to carve a statue of David (the killer of the giant Goliath in the Bible) to symbolise the strength, bravery and freedom of the city. He made one which stood 5.49 m high. It took forty men four days to place it in the main square of Florence. It has now been moved inside the city art gallery and a copy stands in its original place.

Pope Julius II then asked the young Florentine genius back to Rome to make over forty marble statues for a completely over-the-top tomb for himself. Michelangelo was extremely excited by this project and spent over six months in quarries selecting the exact pieces of stone he wanted. But he had hardly begun any carving when he had a big row with the Pope and returned to Florence.

The people of Florence were so worried that the Pope might turn against their city that they persuaded Michelangelo to return to Rome. The Pope then told him to delay work on the tomb and to paint instead the ceiling of the Sistine Chapel in the Vatican City.

Michelangelo was furious and told him fiercely, "I'm *not* a painter, I'm a sculptor!" But the Pope wouldn't listen. They had many arguments but suddenly Michelangelo shut himself up in the chapel in a huff and started to paint. Four years later he emerged with a cricked neck. Alone, he had stood on scaffolding twenty metres above the ground and painted an area the size of a football pitch with over 300 enormous religious figures. He got so used to this position that when he received a letter during this time he had to hold it up and bend his head backwards to read it.

Until recently everyone thought Michelangelo had painted this ceiling in dull colours, but cleaning done nearly 500 years after it was painted shows that he was fond of very bright pinks, greens and yellows and that these had just been covered by centuries of dirt.

Michelangelo was keen to get back to Pope Julius' tomb and started work again on the pieces of stone he had specially chosen. But this project seemed to be jinxed for him because, even though the plans became less and less elaborate, he wasn't able to finish it until 1545 (44 years after it was first commissioned). Julius was long since dead. In the meantime Michelangelo had become so popular that every pope - and many princes - of the time wanted later generations to know that they had commissioned a work by Michelangelo. This kept interrupting the work on the statues for Julius' tomb.

Michelangelo lived to be 88. In later life he got even more tetchy and he was known for his terrible temper. In one rage he, it is believed, hacked off Christ's leg in his Florence *Pietà*. Michelangelo said he had mutilated the work because his servant had nagged him to finish it.

Like Leonardo, Michelangelo also dissected corpses to study them so he could create as real images as possible.

## Raphael (1483-1520)

Raphael also attended a master painter's workshop, that of Perugino in his small home city of Urbino. He arrived in Florence in 1504, at the age of 21, to study the work of the two greatest painters of the day, Leonardo and Michelangelo, and to compete with them. Others were put off by their genius, but not Raphael.

Raphael was a much more friendly person than the other two and got on well with everyone, including his patrons - very important for getting commissions. He painted portraits, frescos and was even an architect. His big breakthrough came in 1508, when he was just 25. Pope Julius II asked him to paint some rooms in the Vatican. Michelangelo was in Rome at the same time, but they didn't get on. Raphael died young, on his 37th birthday, but rich and famous. Apparently the Pope cried bitterly when he was told of Raphael's death.

Until the 19th century Raphael was much better known than Leonardo and Michelangelo in the rest of

Europe. This was because Raphael painted lots of "transportable" pictures - especially of a serene looking Virgin Mary - which were bought by people all over Europe.

# THE RENAISSANCE IN VENICE

The wet, watery city of Venice was another painters' paradise. In the 16th century artists here concentrated on light and colour; in fact they often planned their paintings around the effects of colour.

The dampness from the canals in the city meant frescos here would go mouldy, and wood panels were not great for painting on in a damp place either. So they started to use canvas. A canvas is a woven cloth (the best is linen) which has been stretched on a frame and then coated with a weak glue or gelatine to stop the fabric absorbing the paint. Lots of large canvas paintings still hang in churches in Venice. Paintings on canvas are easier to transport than paintings on wooden panels. Lots of paintings were commissioned in Venice to travel all over Europe.

# TITIAN (c. 1485-1576)

Probably the most famous of all the Venetian painters is Titian. Although he apparently lived to the ripe old age of 99, he is supposed to have lied about his birthday to appear older than he actually was. He seldom drew out a design before he started and he used oil paints (not tempera like in Florence) so he could paint over bits and make changes as he developed a picture. He became a great friend of

Emperor Charles V after he painted a full length portrait of him on horseback. The Emperor then gave him lots of high honours and made him a Count. No artist had ever held such an important position before. In fact there is a story that the great Emperor once picked up a paint brush Titian had dropped! Wow! An emperor bowing before a painter! Everyone who was anyone wanted their portrait painted by Titian.

## TINTORETTO (1518-1594)

Another Venetian painter. *Tintoretto* actually means "little dyer". He got his nickname because of his father's profession (from the Italian word *tintore*, "to dye"). His real name was Jacopo Robusti. Tintoretto and Titian were always in fierce competition for work.

### POISONOUS PAINTS

Some of the paints the Venetian painters used were very poisonous. To get bright yellow or red colours they used arsenic sulphides (but even so the yellow was not as bright as yellows today). No wonder the artists at this time had lots of assistants to do the dirty work, like mixing paint - it was a matter of life or death!

## MANNERISM AND THE LATE RENAISSANCE

*or "Watch your Ps and Qs!"*

The term *Renaissance* is used to describe paintings until about 1600. But even before this, as always with art, some artists reacted to what had gone previously -

this time to the perfection of the High Renaissance painters. The *Mannerists* used the style of the Renaissance, but painted figures with long bodies and limbs. They ignored the rules of perspective and didn't worry about what size a person or a building in the background should be. Many of their figures were twisted in bizarre, impossible positions. The first art historian Vasari (see page 72) praised the style, but later critics attacked it, saying the Mannerists distorted the achievements and work of the great artists of the High Renaissance. The term Mannerism was actually coined in the 1920s but comes from the Italian *maniera*, meaning "style" or "stylishness".

## A EUROPEWIDE RENAISSANCE

Elsewhere in Europe artists were trying out the new discoveries of the Renaissance period (see p52). Portraits became very popular. Towards the end of the period in England a painter called *Hilliard* (1547-1619) did miniatures of people. Some people wore these as jewellery, maybe as a brooch or a pendant. Elizabeth I used to give miniatures of herself to loyal subjects. They were always of her as a young woman (well, what woman gives away pictures of herself as an old hag!).

In Spain the Greek artist (from the island of Crete actually) *El Greco* (1541-1614) - meaning "the Greek" in Spanish - painted elongated figures in his pictures. Some say that this was because he was a Mannerist in style, others that it was because he had an astigmatism (faulty vision which meant he saw distorted images).

Others say he is a Baroque artist (see next section). El Greco always signed his work with his real name in Greek characters *(Domenikos Theotocopoulos)*.

## THE SALT CELLAR MAN

*Benvenuto Cellini* (1500-71), a goldsmith from Florence and a Mannerist sculptor, is most famous for a gold salt cellar which he made for the king of France (Francis I, the same one that Leonardo worked for). It is 34 cm wide, 27 cm high and has the god Neptune as the sea holding the salt and a woman representing the Earth on it. She holds the pepper which comes from a shrub that grows on land.

## THAT'S NOT A FACE, IT'S A TURNIP!

*Giuseppe Arcimboldo* (1527-93) an artist from Milan in Italy, painted faces made up of vegetables, fruit and flowers and landscapes arranged into human forms. He had begun his career designing stained-glass windows for Milan Cathedral.

## ART HISTORY

In 1550 an Italian artist called *Giorgio Vasari* (1511-74) published a book entitled *The Lives of the Most Eminent Italian Artists, Painters and Sculptors*. Much of what we know about the Renaissance artists and others before them comes from this book.

He himself was a Mannerist painter. Modern research into painters of this time shows that Vasari left out people he didn't like, even if they were good artists! Maybe he should have called it *The Lives of My Friends*!

# THE AGE OF BAROQUE

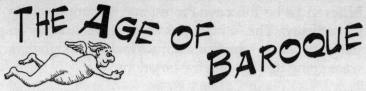

In the 17th century in Europe there were lots of styles and approaches to art but in general much of the work of this period is referred to as *Baroque*.

In fact the word Baroque wasn't actually used until after the period and was meant to be an insult! It really means irregularly-shaped, grotesque or odd. It comes from the Portuguese word for a rough or misshapen pearl, *barrocco*.

Later critics used this term because they thought that 17th century architects had lacked taste and had abused the strict rules used to build Ancient Greek and Roman buildings. They thought they were too free and independent in their designs.

The term was also applied in general to many artists and sculptors of the time.

## ONE BAROQUE STYLE – ENERGETIC, PASSIONATE AND THEATRICAL.

Many paintings and statues of the Baroque period were very theatrical with lots of energy and passion. This style was probably developed because the Catholic Church wanted a strong contrast to what they believed to be the new Protestant  approach to Christianity. The sculptor *Bernini* (1598-1680) - an Italian of course - made his statues look as though they were going through intense emotions.

These Baroque artists took reality further than the Renaissance artists and painted people in an even more real way. Some called it *Naturalism*. For example, Christ's disciples look like hard-working fishermen and wear fishermen's clothes, they are not painted as upper class Romans in togas. One artist, *Caravaggio*, used the body of a woman dragged out of a river as a model for a picture of the Virgin Mary. The Church was not at all happy about that approach. As well as religious scenes, Greek and Roman myths were also painted.

THIS SHOULD DO NICELY

## CARAVAGGIO THE CRIMINAL

Caravaggio (1573-1610) was an Italian and the most famous Baroque artist. His paintings were very dramatic. He cleverly contrasted harsh light and deep shadow to make it seem as though the figures were about to erupt out of the frame. He influenced artists all over Europe. He took reality to an extreme - in one of his religious pictures *The Supper at Emmaus*, apples in a bowl on the disciples' supper table seem to be worm-eaten and have dying leaves on them.

The Protestant Church was set up in the 16th century as a protest against the pomp and ceremony of the existing Catholic Church and became particularly popular in northern Europe. The Protestants thought churches should be plain and simple with no paintings on the walls and no statues. Protestants and Catholics are both Christians.

But it was not just Caravaggio's pictures that were full of energy and passion - he was pretty wild himself. In 1606 he had to flee Rome after he had killed a man in an argument over a tennis match (well, not tennis as we know it!). In fact he already had quite a police record by then which ranged from breaking windows to assaulting a waiter. Caravaggio wasn't even his real name - he was actually called Michelangelo Merisi. Caravaggio was the place he was born!

# RUBENS  , THE COMPANY DIRECTOR

The Flemish artist Sir Peter Paul Rubens (1577-1640), who had worked in Italy when young and got some ideas there (like using great big canvases), also had a very dramatic style. He produced an enormous number of pieces of work - more than 3,000 paintings and over 400 drawings in less than 40 years. And he was as involved in the world of politics as he was in the world of art - he was a diplomat and an ambassador and spoke five languages. He also wrote about archeology.

"So how did he find time to paint all those pictures?" you might ask.

---

Rubens usually signed himself *Pietro Pauolo* - Italian for his first two names, Peter Paul.

Well, he didn't paint them all - or at least not on his own. Like all painters of his time, Rubens ran workshops where his assistants were trained to follow his style exactly. Rubens believed that the idea for the layout of a picture was more important than actually doing it. Sometimes he just did a small coloured sketch and then his assistants used a grid system to transfer these ideas on to the big canvas itself. However, before anything left his studio (or "picture factory"?!), Rubens touched it up so he could say he had actually worked on it. It was the only way he could do all the portraits and pieces of work commissioned from him by kings and dukes and other important people.

## ANTHONY VAN DYCK (1599-1641)

One of Rubens' assistants was Anthony van Dyck, another Flemish painter who did a lot of work in England. He painted many portraits of people in England, in particular the King, Charles I. One of his pictures of Charles is enormous and shows him sitting on a horse. You have to look up to look at the King. It's meant to show how important and powerful he was. In fact Charles wasn't really in control of his kingdom at all, and a few years later his Parliament voted to chop off his head. Propaganda, with art or otherwise, doesn't always work!

## VELÁZQUEZ, THE MAN IN SPAIN

The Spanish artist Velázquez (1599-1660) painted himself into his famous, *three metre high*, picture of Margarita, the daughter of King Philip IV. It is called *Las Meninas* meaning "The Maids of Honour" because Margarita is surrounded by attendants, one serving her refreshments. Behind her, and a little to the side, is Velázquez with his enormous canvas. But would he really have been standing there when the picture was painted? In the very background, as though reflected in a mirror, are the top parts of the bodies of the King and Queen standing together. Is Velázquez indicating that he is really painting the royal couple and that Margarita and her gang are really watching him watching her parents? And who is the man looking through the door at the back

of the room? Has he come to check if the adults are all ready for a cup of tea?

What's more, in the background of this picture Velázquez has painted in two pictures by Rubens on the wall.

## ANOTHER BAROQUE STYLE - ILLUSIONISM

Obvious really - painting an illusion, a bit of magic, something that looks very real but isn't. It was often used on ceilings to make them look as though they were open to the sky. Real figures of real gods seemed to float around real clouds. Illusionism was very fashionable in the 17th century.

## MORE BAROQUE STYLES - CALM CLASSICAL LANDSCAPES AND CLASSICAL SCENES

This was a much quieter approach to things. To join the Classical Landscapes club you had to paint Roman ruins and people (often very small) in beautiful scenery (oh yes, you had to use soft colours too). As Rome was the "in place" to hang out for all European artists at this time the scenery in these pictures is often the countryside around Rome itself, or sometimes the artist just invented a "perfect" landscape.

*Claude Lorrain* (1600-82) was one of the main painters in this club. Claude (as he is usually known) actually started life as a pastry cook. His real name was Claude Gellée - he was called Le Lorrain (in French) or Lorraine (in English) - like the quiche! - after the place of his birth.

Another French painter *Nicholas Poussin* (1594-1665) painted classical scenes with large classical figures in them.

## BAROQUE PAINTING IN HOLLAND

Holland became an independent state in the 17th century, 1609 to be very exact. Before it had been owned by Spain and was part of the Netherlands. Now it was free and independent and had a lot of rich merchants. This was very important because, as it was also Protestant, the churches didn't order paintings as they did in Catholic countries. Religious painting, in general, was frowned upon here.

But that didn't matter because there were lots of very wealthy merchants in the new capital of Amsterdam to buy portraits and other pictures. As well as portraits they wanted scenes of everyday life (maybe a room in someone's house - these rooms always seemed to be tidy!), scenes with farm animals (like hens, cows and sheep), scenes of flat Dutch landscapes (with no people and lots of sky), scenes of the sea (also with lots of sky - and sea of course, and some ships) and still-life subjects (like fruit and flowers).

However Dutch merchants had little tradition of actually commissioning pictures (unlike the Catholic Church and rich aristocrats) so many Dutch artists painted their pictures before they had a buyer - as an artist would usually do today - and then tried to sell them at markets and elsewhere. Although many middle-class Dutch people could now afford to buy paintings for their homes, it was still difficult for some artists to make a living. Some tried to get their names well-known by becoming a specialist in a particular area, other had to do another job as well. Wheeler-dealers began to emerge in the Dutch art world, buying up paintings from artists and then selling them on to their contacts at a profit. The Dutch artist *Jan Vermeer* (1632-75) not only painted but also dealt in pictures - and was probably an innkeeper too!

## REMBRANDT

Rembrandt van Rijn (1606-1669) is the most famous Dutch painter from this time. He is one of the few Dutch artists who did paint pictures of Bible stories and scenes from classical mythology. Rembrandt used light and darkness to great effect in these pictures and he seems to have been able to paint people's feelings in their movements. But he really earned his living by painting portraits of wealthy Dutch people.

Rembrandt was a commoner (though he did have a rich wife), but he seems to have had an enormous ego and was probably a bit of a social climber as well. He painted over 70 portraits of himself and in many of them he is wearing the clothes of a nobleman - velvet cloaks and gold chains - or is surrounded by items associated with the aristocracy. In fact he even shows himself coming back from a successful hunt - very upper-class!

## FRANS HALS

One of the most well known paintings by Dutch artist *Frans Hals* (1581-1666) is of a drunk mad woman talking to a parrot. In this picture he too uses light and dark to great effect.

## SUMMING UP BAROQUE - IF THAT'S POSSIBLE!

Well, Baroque appears to mean anything vaguely artistic in the 17th century! The term is not only used for art, sculpture and architecture but also for music. Apparently all of Europe at this time was influenced by developments in Italy - even Dutch still lifes! (The "experts" say they were affected by the Naturalism of the best known Baroque artist, Caravaggio (see p74 ).

In fact the term Baroque is used so broadly for art that anyone who didn't just copy the styles of the High Renaissance artists in the 17th century seems to be called a Baroque artist - if you had been painting then you might have been one too!

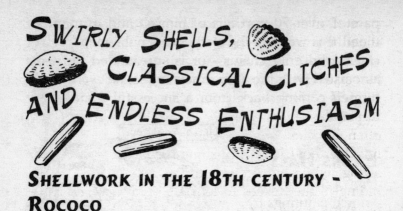

# SWIRLY SHELLS, CLASSICAL CLICHES AND ENDLESS ENTHUSIASM

## SHELLWORK IN THE 18TH CENTURY - ROCOCO

Like Baroque, the name *Rococo* was meant to be a term of abuse! It was first used in the 19th century to describe much of the art and architecture of the first half of the 18th century. It comes from the French word *rocaille* and means *pebbles and shell-work* and was used because a lot of the art of this period was very "squirly" and whirly - very ornate with lots of curves and curls. In the 19th century viewers generally thought it was horrendous, but some people quite like it now.

The Rococo style began in France but then spread throughout Europe. Some people had thought the Baroque style was a bit too pompous. In contrast Rococo was very airy fairy - playful and giggly. Lots of light colours were used, like pale pinks, blues and greens. The paintings were usually of light-hearted activities such as picnics and outdoor parties attended by well-dressed, rich aristocrats.

The French artists *Jean-Antoine Watteau* (1684-1721), *François Boucher* (1703-1770) and *Jean-Honoré Fragonard* (1732-1806) epitomise the fancy, frivolous Rococo style. Boucher is said to have stated that nature was too green and badly-lit to paint as it really was! He also made designs for fans and slippers. Fragonard painted the girl in the famous picture *The Swing* which often appears on chocolate box lids. Her boyfriend is pushing the swing, while her secret admirer is hiding in the bushes to look up her skirts as she soars overhead!

## LOOKING BACK AGAIN,
## 18TH CENTURY STYLE - NEOCLASSICAL

In 1748 the ruins of Pompeii were discovered in Italy. Europe was so excited! Here was an opportunity to time-travel and see what life was really like in ancient Roman times. This Roman town had been smothered by volcanic ash in AD 79 (see p30).

Immediately the pure classical style was back in fashion - none of those fancy Baroque or Rococo approaches to things. New classical, or *Neoclassical*, was "in". The new style was pretty severe and serious - it was just as if a strict school master had said, "Calm down, be a bit more serious towards your work!" Other excavations and discoveries from Ancient Greece and Rome influenced this trend still more.

Neoclassical is another term to describe a period of artistic style which was originally meant as a term of abuse! In the mid 19th century, when the style had gone out of fashion, the term was invented to apply to

Classically-inspired works which, to 19th century critics, seemed lifeless and impersonal.

## Daaaaaaaaaa-veed

The most famous artist of this period was a Frenchman, Jacques-Louis David (1748-1825), (pronounced with a French accent, *Daaaaaaaaaa-veed*). David painted lots of pictures with figures from Roman history and Roman myths. He was influenced by Poussin and, like Poussin, David's style was quite serious and sombre.

David lived at an adventurous time in France - and had to use all his cunning to survive being killed. This was the time of the French Revolution and in 1793 the French people cut off the head of their king, Louis XVI. David was in total support of this. He then became *the* painter of the French Revolution.

But currents change swiftly during revolutions and David suddenly found himself imprisoned. He was only released because his ex-wife, who had divorced him for voting for the execution of King Louis, pleaded for him. As a way of thanks David re-married her. He then managed to worm himself into the affections of the new French leader, Napoleon, and became the Emperor's official painter. He flattered Napoleon, for example in the picture *The Coronation of*

*Napoleon and Josephine* he made Napoleon appear larger than life-size (in real life Napoleon was a titch!).

David was now the most influential artist in Europe. It is said that if he painted a lady in a certain style of dress, all the fashionable people in Paris were soon wearing it. But his influences were not just in fashion. He helped to start up special Academies of Art in many capital cities of Europe to teach strict rules to younger artists. His influence was so great in fact that he banned any new artists who did not paint "properly", often wrecking their careers.

## THE GRAND TOUR

In the 18th century it became fashionable for gentlemen to spend up to a year travelling around Europe as part of their education. If they had had cameras they would have been endlessly snapping the interesting places they visited; as they didn't they bought paintings. These paintings were specially produced for the tourist industry and some were more accurate than others. Sometimes there might be two, or even more, sights in the picture, even though really only one could be seen from that location. Venice was a particularly popular tourist destination, probably because of the canals and gondoliers and therefore the Venetian, *Canaletto* (1697-1768), was probably the most famous view painter of the 18th century. Appropriately his real name was *Mr Canal* (Giovanni Antonio Canale)!

The smart travellers on the Grand Tour were also keen to view the art of Europe. They visited private collections that had been built up by rich individuals. Often they came back with art objects from the countries they visited. A lot of these countries now regard these particular items as plundered.

## EXHIBITIONS

Art was a really "in" thing in the 18th century. As more and more people became interested in it, societies were founded to set up exhibitions of paintings for members to look at. Some of these were later opened to the public. The first real modern "people's" museum was the Louvre in Paris. After the French Revolution, in 1793, this former royal palace was opened to the public. It contained the amazing collections of art which the French royal family had owned (including Leonardo's *Mona Lisa*, see p63).

## BRITAIN - PEOPLE AND ANIMALS

Portraits, of both people and animals, were very popular in Britain in the 18th century. The three main English portrait painters were:

### WILLIAM HOGARTH (1697-1764)

Hogarth did not just paint portraits, he also painted various series of pictures that told moral stories, like "don't have too much of the good life", in a theatrical way. Engravings were made from the original oil paintings and they were very popular with all classes of people. In fact, Hogarth had originally been apprenticed to an engraver, but had fallen out with him when he had eloped with the guy's daughter!

## SIR JOSHUA REYNOLDS (1723-92)

Some say Sir Joshua is the most important person in the history of English painting. He was the first President of the Royal Academy of Arts in England which was set up in 1768. Reynolds seemed to be able to put the individuality of the sitters into his portraits.

## THOMAS GAINSBOROUGH (1727-88)

Gainsborough loved the countryside and would rather have painted that than portraits, but English patrons only really wanted to buy pictures of themselves. His portrait of *Mr and Mrs Andrews* is believed to be unfinished, as, if you look closely, there is the outline of a bird in Mrs Andrews' lap - perhaps it was to be a pheasant that Mr Andrews had shot (he is shown standing with a shotgun and a dog). Maybe Mrs Andrews put her foot down and said that she didn't want a dead bird lying in her lap in the picture.

## GEORGE STUBBS (1724-1806)

George Stubbs was a popular painter of animals at this time, especially horses. It's hardly surprising he painted horses well, because he really, really studied them to make sure he got them right. This is how he did it. Over a two year period, Stubbs used to have a dead horse hanging from the ceiling of his cottage for about two months at a time so he could study and draw it! (The blood would have been drained out of the dead horse first and then the veins filled with liquid wax.)

He published his book of engravings, *Anatomy of the Horse*, in 1759. It is still one of the best on horses.

# ROMANTICS AND REALISTS

## ROMANTICS

Well, needless to say, young painters at the end of the 18th century and at the beginning of the 19th century got a bit tired of David and the other Neoclassicists telling them how to paint. Many of the new generation acted against the strict rules of the Art Academies of the European cities and started to paint in a way that showed their own feelings more. They later became known as the *Romantics*. The approach of the Romantics was very different from the strictness of the Neoclassicists.

And Italy was no longer at the centre of painting - Paris was now the place to be!

## FRANCE

*Géricault* (1791-1824), was a popular Romantic artist. His most famous work is *The Raft of the Medusa*.

The Medusa was a French ship which sank in 1816 off West Africa. The Captain and the senior officers got into the only two lifeboats. The other 150 people (including the rest of the crew and one woman) hastily put together a raft to be towed by the lifeboats. But the others rowed off.

BYE! HA! HA!

"What now? What now?" cried those on the raft, as they fortified themselves on their only provisions - casks of wine.

Ten days later they saw a ship, the "Argus", but it didn't see them and sailed on by. It was another five days before the few survivors saw the "Argus" again. This time it did spot them, and the 15 remaining people on the raft were rescued.

Géricault's picture of this horrendous adventure is enormous - 7.16 m by 4.91 m. He interviewed survivors, had a model of the raft built, and also went to the morgue to look at corpses! Géricault was determined to make his picture as realistic as possible.

Géricault had a big influence on the most famous Romantic artist, Delacroix, and the two men became great friends. In fact Delacroix modelled for one of the figures in Géricault's *Raft of the Medusa* (he's the dead young man in the centre foreground, lying facedown).

Géricault was also into painting horses but ironically he died falling from a horse at the tender age of 33.

*Delacroix* (1798-1863) was the most famous of the Romantic artists. He thought the use of bright, strong colours (he got some of his ideas on a visit to Morocco and also by looking at Rubens' work) was more important than exactness of detail. Delacroix began to get more official commissions than David's neoclassical pupil, Ingres. Delacroix's work became very popular and in 1855, at the Paris World Exhibition, he had 36 of his pieces hanging in one room. After he died, over 9,000 pictures and sketches were found in his studio.

*Ingres* (1780-1867). Actually this man is in the wrong section! His style was neoclassical but it just goes to show that everything is not cut and dried in art; the old style keeps going alongside the new. Ingres was David's star pupil, and like him was influenced by the serious style of Poussin. Ingres was a popular artist too and he and Delacroix were always in competition with each other - in fact a caricaturist of the time did a picture of them fighting each other, Ingres holding a pencil and Delacroix a paintbrush!

## GERMANY

*Friedrich* (1774-1840) was the most famous German Romantic painter. He painted lots of landscapes, some with crosses and Gothic ruins in them - very eerie!

## SPAIN

*Goya* (1746-1828) France invaded Spain during Goya's life so he painted lots of the cruel deeds of war. He was really doing what war photographers do today, recording it all. He was also court painter to the Spanish court. He went completely deaf in the middle of his life after a mystery illness. Apparently Goya always painted by daylight, but had a hat with candles on it so he could touch up his pictures in the evening. He wanted to create the effect of what they would look like by candlelight!

## CHANGES IN PAINT

Painters in the early 19th century had a major advantage over earlier artists. They could pack up their paints, make up a picnic and set off wherever they liked to paint, paint, paint. This was because some, like the English artist Turner, now used watercolours a lot. A small box of watercolours, some brushes and the paper were easily carried, whereas oil paints had to be mixed and then used quickly. Later in the century - about 1840 - collapsible tubes were invented and painters could then use almost any type of paint anywhere they liked. Watercolours are so called because to make them lighter you just dilute them with water so more light from the white paper underneath is seen. Watercolour is difficult to paint with because it dries too quickly to correct mistakes! (Like the old tempera).

## ENGLAND

*Turner* (1775-1851) was once accused of painting a picture that looked like "soapsuds and whitewash". *Snowstorm: Steamship off a Harbour's Mouth* was actually meant to be a steamship in a snowstorm. Turner had put a lot of Romantic style feeling and emotion in to it. Maybe this has contributed to the myth that has grown up around the painting, that in order to get the atmosphere as accurate as possible Turner had himself tied to the mast of a ship as it journeyed along in a bad storm - and stayed there for four hours!

A lot of people didn't like Turner's work because he painted the atmosphere of a scene rather than the exact details of it. He even annoyed people who liked his paintings - if he had paintings hanging in an exhibition, he used to rush in to put finishing touches to them hours before the exhibition opened! Turner became more and more of a recluse in his later life. He died in a London boarding house where he had been staying under the name of Mr Booth.

*Constable* (1776-1837) was also a keen painter of the English countryside, particularly Suffolk where he grew up. He once said, "The sound of water escaping from mill dams, willows, old rotten planks, slimy posts and brickwork, I love such things. These scenes made me a painter."

Constable also once said, "Another word for painting is feeling."

## REALISTS

Towards the middle of the 19th century another approach to painting became popular in France. These painters were called the *Realists*. The Realists didn't agree with using the imagination to paint a picture. They thought everything should be painted exactly as it looked - like a photograph in fact. The Realists often chose to paint ordinary people at their totally unromantic everyday tasks.

One of the most famous of the Realists' pictures was destroyed in World War II in a bombing raid on Dresden in Germany, where it hung in a gallery, and, ironically, we only have photographs of it now. It was called *The Stonebreakers* and was by the Frenchman, *Courbet* (1819-1877). *The Stonebreakers* was of men doing the hard, manual work of breaking up stones, which had to be done by hand before the days of machines. Critics thought this was not a subject worth painting. (Apparently when Courbet was once asked to include angels in a picture he was doing for a church, he replied: "I have never seen an angel. Show me an angel and I will paint one".)

## THE PRE-RAPHAELITE BROTHERHOOD

When some pictures were exhibited in London in 1849 signed with the initials "PRB", people asked questions. The Pre-Raphaelite Brotherhood was a very small "secret" society made up of some artists who were inspired by the style of art *before* the Italian Renaissance painter Raphael. The PRBs believed art should be serious and moral. They tended to use bright colours on a white background and they loved painting women.

Beware of anyone with a nice, gentle family sounding name like Dadd. The English painter *Richard Dadd* (1817-86) killed his own dad in a fit of madness in 1843 and spent the rest of his life in asylums - where he painted most of his best work.

# IMPRESSIONISTS

Art historians disagree about when "modern" art began. Some say it was with the Impressionists in the second part of the 19th century.

## IMPRESSIONISTS

Watch it! This is yet another rude word!

The first time the term *Impressionists* was used it was meant to be an insult! An art critic used it to describe the artists of an exhibition of paintings in 1874 in Paris. He made a joke of the title of a painting by one of them, Monet, *Impression: Sunrise*. Along with quite a few other people, the critic didn't like the new style of paintings in this exhibition. But the new artists quite liked the joke name and decided to use it themselves!

So who or what were the Impressionists? Did they go round pulling faces and doing impressions of things and getting  their friends to paint them? No, they actually used light and colour to give an impression of something, rather than painting it exactly. A bit like the Romantics, you might think? Yes, but no! As seems to be the norm with all young artists, these ones wanted to be different from the ones which had gone just before - the Impressionists said that the Romantics had got too emotionally involved in their pictures, and had created just the idea of the "general" atmosphere of something. The Impressionists wanted to convey an impression of something in a split second of time, as if you were looking at it there and then. A second later the light might be very different. This meant they had a good excuse for painting the same thing again and again ...

*Monet* (1840-1926), for example, painted the same haystack several times, also the railway station of St Lazare in Paris several times, the west side of Rouen Cathedral several times, and he did endless pictures of the water-lilies in his garden pond . In fact he was so obsessed by getting his water-lilies exactly right that he is said to have employed a special gardener whose only job was to stop leaves falling into the pond! The different effect of the light during various times of the day was what really interested him.

One of Monet's earlier pictures, *The Beach at Trouville*, which he painted while on holiday, has tiny bits of sand and shell stuck to it. He was obviously actually painting it on the beach in a gusty breeze - very different from the studio approaches of the past.

---

Monet gave several of his water-lily pictures to the Louvre in Paris as a war memorial picture after World War One.

*Manet* (1832-1883) was one of the first of this new style of painters to really annoy the picture viewing public. In fact Paris was shocked! Women probably needed smelling salts at the mere thought of his picture *Déjeuner sur l'herbe* ("Lunch on the Grass") which showed one naked woman and one nearly naked sitting having a picnic with two clothed men. People could cope with the traditional pictures of everyone having no clothes on at all, or everyone fully dressed ... but the two mixed together?! Terrible!! Critics also said the picture was badly painted - if you stand closer than about a metre you can often easily see the brush strokes of an Impressionist picture. Also the Impressionists tended to use a contrasting colour instead of a defining line. This, too, went against the traditional style of painting.

Manet's picnic picture was rejected from the main art exhibition in Paris in 1863 so he, and others who had had their work rejected, then exhibited their pictures in the *Salon des Refusés* or the "Salon of the Rejected Painters". Ironically, Impressionist pictures now sell for thousands of pounds and are often bought to make money, not just because people like them.

Manet obviously spent a lot of his time hanging out in Paris cafés because they feature a lot in his paintings.

Other Impressionist painters who hung out in Paris in the 1860s, 70s and 80s were:

*Pissarro* (1830-1903) was the only impressionist artist to exhibit in all eight of their exhibitions. Born in the West Indies, he moved to France in 1855. He painted lots of pictures of peasants. However, from about 1895 his eyesight deteriorated and so he had to give up painting out of doors and used to paint views of Paris from windows in the city. He died blind.

*Degas* (1834-1917) was also French. He painted many scenes of "behind the scenes" at the ballet, the horse-racing, the theatre and the circus - as well as scenes in French cafés, of course. He liked what appeared to be unposed scenes, like a ballet dancer doing up her shoe in the rehearsal room. He also made sculptures - one of these, *Little Fourteen-year-old Dancer* (1881), is dressed in a real tutu.

*Mary Cassett* (1844-1926) was American but also hung out with the Impressionists in the Paris cafés. She was very good at painting scenes of women and children (although she had no children of her own). She was also keen on making prints and was very influenced by Japanese art (see p100).

*Berthe Morisot* (1841-95) was a grand-daughter of the French Rococo painter Fragonard (see p82). She was French too and was very influenced by Manet (who was also her brother-in-law). She used to pose for him a lot.

*Renoir* (1841-1919), also French, began his working life painting porcelain in a Paris factory. One of his pictures *The Umbrellas* shows how he experimented with different styles over the years. He probably started it in 1880-81 and finished it in 1886. Not only are there two different painting styles in the picture, (first - feathery brush strokes for the two little girls on the right; second - a sharper approach for the figures on the left), but the fashions of the clothes they are wearing are from different years!

*Whistler* (1834-1903) was born in America but spent a lot of time in France and England. A famous art critic, called John Ruskin, accused him of "flinging a pot of paint in the public face" because he thought one of Whistler's paintings was so horrendous. Whistler took Ruskin to court for being rude about him ... and won! But Whistler was only awarded a farthing and became bankrupt because of the costs of the fight with Ruskin. Whistler's most famous painting is of his mother.

*Rodin* (1840-1917) was a very, very famous French sculptor. Sometimes, however, his work didn't look as though it was quite "finished" - or so the general public thought. He perhaps would leave part of the original stone attached to the sculpture so it would look as though it was just developing from the piece of marble (or whatever the material was). His piece *The Hand of God* ➤ is like this. Some viewers accused him of being lazy with his work when they saw it!

## MODERN ADVANCES FOR PAINTERS

❈ *Portable paints*: The Impressionists were able to make use of new types of paints made of chemicals, and the new portable squeezy metal tubes they were in, to get out of doors to paint scenes actually on the spot rather than from sketches inside a studio. Up to now artists, or their assistants, had had to prepare all the paint in their studios.

❈ *Ideas about colour:* They also used new observations about colour, for example green appears to be in the shadow of a red object, orange in that of a blue object. As well as all this the Impressionists had the advantage of new research in the 19th century into how optical illusions could be created by placing different colours next to each other. For example red and yellow beside each other make your eyes think you are looking at orange.

❈ *Photography:* The Impressionists often used the exciting invention of the camera (a process for making photographic images was discovered in 1839). They could now take photographs which showed how light and shadows would change and could make an object look very different. (Remember, these early photographs were black and white.)

## INFLUENCES FROM JAPAN

The work of Japanese artists had a great influence on European artists at this time, especially the Impressionists like Mary Cassett. 18th and 19th century Japanese artists made coloured prints from carved woodblocks of the daily lives of ordinary people, such as fishermen.

*Hokusai* (1760-1849) was one of the great experts at this. He, and others, also made pictures of lovely landscapes with parts of the view blocked by the activities in the foreground - like his picture of a man with a machine drawing water in front of Mount Fuji, Japan's most famous and highest mountain. These made the European artists realise that, as an artist, you can block some of the most important parts of something out of a picture, but, if you hint at it, the viewer's imagination will put the rest of it back in. A lot of early western European advertising pictures were influenced by this idea too.

*Wrapping paper*: Many of the Japanese prints which influenced European artists arrived in Europe as wrapping paper for other goods being imported from Japan!

## PHOTOGRAPHING HORSES

It was only in the late 19th century that artists started painting accurate pictures of moving horses. This was because the photographer *Eadweard Muybridge* (1830-1904) published sequences of photographs which showed that a trotting horse, and also a galloping horse, could have all four feet off the ground at once. He set up a series of cameras along the edge of racetracks to take these photographs. Degas and other painters of horses were very influenced by them.

## ARCHITECTURE

The Industrial Revolution influenced developments in architectural design and building materials in Europe at this time. In London, the enormous *Crystal Palace* was built of glass for the Great Exhibition of 1851. It was like a gigantic greenhouse!

In Paris the 300 metre high iron *Eiffel Tower* was prefabricated in a factory and then erected in March 1889 for the Paris Exhibition (it was named after its designer, M. Eiffel). Unfortunately for nearly the first two months the lifts didn't work so visitors had to climb all the way to the top!

### A QUICK QUESTION!

What do you think the colour of water is? Blue? Green? Grey? Blue and green? Grey and blue? Pink and green? The Impressionists spent a lot of time trying to work that out - as have many artists before and since. Check it out yourself. Look at water and look at paintings to see what colour artists have shown it!

# POST-IMPRESSIONISM

This fancy phrase just means "After Impressionism". Well, obviously everything that has happened in the art world since the late 19th century is "After Impressionism", but in art terms the phrase just refers to a few years and a few artists at the end of the 19th century and the very beginning of the 20th century. The artists known as the Post-Impressionists never used the term themselves (in fact they were almost all dead by the time it was first used at an exhibition of their pictures in 1910!). The Post-Impressionists were influenced by the Impressionists but often used much stronger colours. They each developed their own styles, which in turn influenced later painters. Some of the Post-Impressionists lived in the south of France where the strong, bright sun does make everything seem very, very bright to look at.

*Van Gogh* (1853-90) was a Dutchman who ended up living in the south of France. He is probably most famous for the fact that he cut off part of his left ear after a row with another painter, Gauguin. He then painted a picture of himself with the bandaged ear (and wearing a hat!). He imaginatively called it *Self-Portrait with a Bandaged Ear.*

Van Gogh painted everyday things, like his bed or his chair, in very bright colours - as well as pictures of landscapes. He didn't always copy the colours of a scene exactly, but would try to use the colours to provoke emotions, like happiness, sadness, loneliness. He felt art was a personal thing, not a public thing.

Bright, bright yellow was his favourite colour - when he was in a good mood. He once wrote in a letter to his brother Theo, "What a lovely colour yellow is!" He only sold one painting in his lifetime. A hundred years later, in 1987, his painting *Sunflowers* (lots of bright yellows, of course!) sold for around £20,000,000. Vincent van Gogh once worked for a while as a religious preacher in Belgium, before he moved to the south of France.

*Gauguin* (1848-1903) was a Frenchman but grew up in Peru where his mother came from. He first worked as a stockbroker and just did some painting as a hobby. He was very impressed by the Impressionists and so started painting full time, giving up his seriously well-paid job. He became very poor and had difficulty supporting his family. His paintings were almost like stained glass windows - each feature had a strong outline, and there were big flat areas of the same colour. In 1891 he went to the Pacific island of Tahiti, leaving his family behind. He thought art in Europe was too superficial and wanted to find simplicity. Gaugin's painting had a great influence on later artists.

*Cézanne* (1839-1906) was another Frenchman. He painted endless pictures of apples and other fruit. He also painted landscapes - in fact there was one mountain near where he lived, Mont Sainte-Victoire, that he painted endlessly. He didn't paint the scene exactly as it was at that split second in time, as Manet did, but simplified his pictures by painting the mountain, and other things, as geometric shapes with bold blocks of colour.

*Seurat* (1859-91), a Frenchman too, was dotty about dots. He studied colours and discovered that if you painted lots and lots and lots of small dots of different colours together they almost mix before your eyes to create a shimmering effect. This method of painting is called *pointillism*. He painted various pictures using this technique - a lady powdering her nose, people standing by a river and a circus scene among other things. In fact some art historians refer to Seurat as a *Neo-Impressionist*, a "New Impressionist". The Neo-Impressionists apparently were the ones who used this scientific approach to dots - but Seurat was the only one of them who was any good at it!

# WESTERN ART IN THE MODERN WORLD

## "WEIRD, WONDERFUL AND WACKY"

or so some people think!

Since the Impressionists, artists in the West have not stopped trying new techniques and ideas. They have often been influenced by art from other parts of the world, such as African sculpture. Western artists have tried to paint the inside of the mind (which some artists elsewhere have been doing for centuries!) and have even made sculptures out of chocolate! They have attempted to represent extreme emotions like anger and have exhibited dead sheep! So what is Modern Western Art? Can all of it really be called Art? Even the experts can't decide!

The following are all words to drop into the conversation if you want to impress people with your knowledge of Modern Art:

So what on earth do these "-ism" words actually mean?

## CUBISM

Easy! Painting
everything to look like
cubes! Yes, literally
everything - people,
animals, bottles - were
all made out of cubes.
The Spanish artist
*Picasso* (1881-1973)
developed this
new approach
with his friend
*Braque* (1882-1963).

Braque once said, "The function of art is to
disturb. Science reassures."

## EXPRESSIONISM

Quite easy too! This involves expressing extreme
emotions and feelings in pictures. Everything in the
picture, not just the subject matter, but the colour and
style as well, must contribute to this. The picture *The
Scream* by the Norwegian artist *Munch* (1863-1944) is
an example of this. A lone woman is screaming, her
head is a weird shape, she has her hands over her ears.
She looks as though she is standing on a bridge over a
river. The picture is painted in different, colour
clashing, lines which all lead to her head and this gives
a hysterical feel to the picture. You can almost hear the
scream. *Aaaaargh!*

## SURREALISM

The meaning of this word is *beyond the real*. Artists painted weird dream-like pictures (maybe with floating shapes rather than identifiable objects) and also painted real things in an odd way (like a telephone with a lobster as the receiver!). The Surrealists wanted to make people think about things buried deep in their minds. The Spanish painter *Dali* (1904-89), who painted the lobster telephone, often painted his dreams. Dali was seriously weird himself, and was also a real showman! He once gave a lecture in a deep sea diver's suit (one of the old-fashioned ones with a goldfish bowl helmet) and nearly suffocated. In fact it was not really worth the effort as no one could hear him anyway! He was also famous for his long moustache which curled up at the ends. He was very proud of it and said he could receive messages from space with it because it worked like an antenna!

## PABLO PICASSO

*(1881 Spain-1973 France) Painter, sculptor, costume designer ...*

If Picasso's uncle hadn't smoked, Picasso, probably the most famous artist in the 20th century, might never have lived! When he was born the nurse thought he was dead, but luckily his uncle, who was a doctor, blew cigarette smoke into his face to make him cough and cry!

Picasso's father, José Ruiz Blasco, was an art teacher in a local school. He recognised his son's talent and hoped the boy would become a great artist. As you've noticed, Picasso's name was different from his father's. He used his mother's maiden name. In his teens Picasso applied to Barcelona's School of Fine Arts. He was given a month to do a number of drawings as an entrance exam. He completed them in one day!

After his best friend committed suicide, Picasso painted everything in blue from 1901-4. His father didn't approve. In 1904 Picasso moved to Paris. When he met a girl called Fernande his Blue Period finished as he fell in love. More colour now came in to his paintings - this was the Rose Period and included circus pictures.

Next was Cubism - everything in his pictures were all made out of cubes, including humans. You could see the back of the object in the picture at the same time as the front, not to mention the sides! Not surprising many people were rather shocked by these paintings and didn't like them. This was the first time for hundreds of years artists hadn't tried to paint things so that they looked real. In portraits, too, Picasso used cubist effects. A painting of his daughter Maya with her doll has her eyes, nose and mouth in odd places. But pause a minute - if you think of someone, or something, do you see in your mind the person, or the object, just from the front?

One of Picasso's most famous paintings is *Guernica*. This was called after a town in northern Spain which had been destroyed by bombs during the Spanish Civil War (1936-9). Thousands of innocent people were killed or injured. Picasso wanted to show how terrible war was. The painting was enormous, four metres high and seven metres wide. Picasso filled it with cubism and lots of dark colours. It is an angry, expressive piece of work. It hung in New York's Museum of Modern Art for many years, but now it has been returned to Spain. The move was called *Operation Big Picture*.

Picasso was also a sculptor, but he didn't make traditional stone sculptures. His *Head of a Bull* is made from the saddle and handlebars of a bicycle, *Goat* is a wicker basket, a palm branch, scrap iron and clay pots, while in *Baboon with Young* the baboon's head is made from a toy motor car. Picasso loved junk and collected wire, rope, newspapers, rocks, stones, fossils, bones, toys, masks, ornaments, postcards and other items for his sculptures and for his collages. Picasso was also a costume designer. He created exciting colourful costumes for several ballets performed by a Russian company.

Picasso liked to keep working on his pictures for months or even years. He didn't often feel a picture was finished.

# OTHER ART MOVEMENTS

These ones don't end in -ism!

## THE "WILD BEASTS"

One group was called the *Fauves* which is French for savage "wild beasts". A French art critic said the paintings at an exhibition in 1905 looked as though they had been painted by wild things! The pictures were full of bright, clashing colours used in an unnatural sort of way. For example half the face of a person might be painted green. A Frenchman, *Matisse (1869-54)* was the most famous of this group. He was not interested in using the *right* colours in his pictures, but was more concerned about getting the *right balance* of colours, patterns and shapes. Matisse's first career was as a lawyer.

## ABSTRACT PAINTERS

The term "abstract" usually refers to 20th century art which does not imitate nature. Abstract paintings work like music - they affect the emotions and the mind. Therefore, the artists said a painting didn't always have to look like something that we can recognise. It's how it makes us feel that matters.

*Paul Klee* (1879-1940) was Swiss. He used a lot of geometrical shapes in his pictures. His picture *Senecio* suggests a face and is made up of circles, squares, triangles and other shapes. He was also influenced by children's art and tribal art (see p118).

*Jackson Pollock* (1912-56) was an American artist who placed huge canvases on the floor and then walked across them dripping paint from the can as he went. He next used anything but brushes to work on it - sometimes knives or sticks. In 1956 a magazine nicknamed him Jack the Dripper. This type of painting is called *Action Painting* as there's lots of action - you splash, pour, or dribble paint on to the canvas. In Action Painting the way the artist paints the picture is as important as what the result is.

## POP ART

Pop art began in New York in the late 1950s. Pop artists used images from modern life in the 20th century - soup tins, Coca-Cola bottles, music posters, advertisements and comics among many other things. The American pop artist *Andy Warhol* (1928-87) first came to the general public's attention when he exhibited stencilled pictures of row upon row of Campbell's soup tins and sculptures of boxes of Brillo soap pads. He later made a six hour film, *The Sleep*, of ... a man sleeping for six hours!

Another American pop artist, *Roy Lichtenstein* (b.1923) has done a lot of work based on comic strips, even including the dots of the printing process in his blow ups.

 A lot of pieces of pop art and other modern art are already disintegrating because of the materials used to make them.

## PERFORMANCE ART

This also developed in the late 1950s and involved artists linking different art forms together in their work, such as theatre and music. The best known is probably a German artist, *Joseph Beuys* (1921-86). One of his most famous pieces of performance art was called *How to Explain Pictures to a Dead Hare* in 1965. For this he carried a dead hare around an exhibition of pictures in a German gallery, explaining the pictures to the hare as he went. Beuys covered his face in honey and gold leaf for this performance!

## INSTALLATIONS

Sounds like something the plumber would do, doesn't it?! This form of art has grown since the 1970s. An installation is something that has been set up, or installed, in a gallery for a specific exhibition. In the 1990s English artist *Damien Hirst* (b.1965) has exhibited a dead sheep in a tank of formaldehyde and an "installation" in which flies' eggs go through a process of hatching into flies only to travel towards the light at the other end of the exhibit to be zapped in a fly zapper.

## CONCEPTUAL ART

Based on the belief that the concept, or idea, matters more than the finished product - even if the final piece looks awful, if the idea was good that's all that matters.

113

# Other Types of Art
## Photography

It's legit! Photos are now art!
But artists often also use photographs
to copy from and get ideas from.

The American artist Andy
Warhol did a very famous
picture of Marlilyn Monroe
by projecting a photograph
on to a silk-screen and
copying it.

The British artist *David Hockney* (b. 1937) has produced photographic collages and, from the mid 1980s, he has also used photocopied prints in his work.

## Computer Art

It's now possible to produce art on computers and there are specific software programs for this. Images and colours can be moved around on the screen and made smaller and larger. Many designers in different industries ranging from fashion to TV use them. Architects use computers too nowadays. Would the great designers and artists of the past have been jealous?

## Art and Nature

Art from twigs, leaves, berries, stones and ice! English artist *Andy Goldsworthy* (b. 1956) makes sculptures and pictures from all of these. He stitches together horse chestnut leaves with grass stalks and makes designs out of blackberry leaves splattered with white bird droppings. He works during the night to create sculptures with broken pieces of ice from a lake top which then melt when the sun comes up. The only lasting record of these is a photograph. He once floated, on a pond, red berries between iris blades which were pinned together with thorns. The fish nibbled at the berries from below and the ducks from above.

> Some people say that some of the best artists are spiders - in the creation of their webs!

## DID YOU KNOW ?..

A Volkswagen car is one of the exhibits which has been on display at the Museum of Modern Art in New York.

When his second wife died, *Lavery* (1856-1951) started painting his first wife, who had been a flower girl and had died years before. Lavery was born and raised in Belfast, Ireland.

★ *Lowry* (1887-1979), was a British painter who painted "matchstick men and matchstick cats and dogs". A hit pop song was made about him! Although he was a successful painter he stayed a rent collector all his life and did his painting in the evenings. Apparently Lowry once said, "Had I not been lonely I should not have seen what I did."

★ *Keith Haring* (1958-1990) became a successful American artist. However he began his art career painting graffiti in the subways of New York. When the police came he used to have himself videoed being arrested! He considered this part of his art!

★ *Nolan* (1917-1992) was a famous Australian artist. His most well-known paintings are of the Australian folk hero, Ned Kelly, a bushranger (bandit) who was hanged for his deeds in 1880. Ned was only 26. He had always worn a black box-type metal helmet on his head and Nolan used this to great effect in his 27 pictures of the story. Ned and his gang robbed banks and fought the authorities, but were always friendly to ordinary people.

★ *Whiteley* (1939-1992), was an Australian artist who led a wild lifestyle. One picture of his is called *Self-portrait After 3 Bottles of Wine*. He looks very happy in it. However he probably had a very bad hangover the next day!

*Christo (Christo Javacheff,* b. 1935) is a Bulgarian-born sculptor and designer who now lives in New York. He has "wrapped" various items ranging from trees and cars to enormous structures like the Reichstag, the German parliament building in Berlin. He has also covered "areas" such as thousands of square metres of the Australian coastline in 1969-70 (in plastic sheeting!).

> Modern printing methods have made it possible for ordinary people to own famous works of art - perhaps you have one in your house as a poster or print or table mat!

## THE TURNER PRIZE

This prize is awarded annually for "the greatest contribution to art in Britain in the previous twelve months". The Tate Gallery in London (named after Sir Henry Tate - who made a fortune from inventing the sugar cube) administers it.

There is often controversy about the winners. For example ...

* a pile of bricks

* a plastercast of the inside of a house.

* an hour long video of policemen and policewomen trying to remain as still as possible (they were in a typical formal group photographic pose - half sitting on chairs, half standing behind).

# TRIBAL INFLUENCES

It's only in the 20th century that people in the West have really realised what amazing pieces of art have always been produced in the rest of the world - paintings, carvings, sculptures, buildings; not to mention items made from other types of material such as cloth, grass and straw.

Some western artists in the late 19th century began to look elsewhere for influence, such as the French artist Gauguin, who actually went to live in the island of Tahiti in the South Pacific (see p104). Picasso (see p107) was also very inspired by carvings and sculptures from other cultures, and used many of these ideas in his work.

As many tribal pieces were made for a specific - often religious, ceremonial, or magical - purpose and were not meant to last for future generations to view, there are few very old examples of masks, totem poles, painted pieces of bark, decorated hunting hooks or shields.

However, often the modern products are based on the old traditional types of designs and styles. In some parts of the world these are now dying out as so-called "civilisation" reaches these peoples - but some of the traditional approaches are still surviving.

## CARVED AND PAINTED MASKS

Carved and painted masks from around the world are very beautiful and can show an intense range of emotions with only a few cuts of the knife. Masks can be made to represent animals or gods, or can show the status of a figure in a ceremony. They are often intended to frighten away evil spirits, to encourage rain to fall, or to make the fishing better. Different colour paints can mean different things in different cultures. Depending on the part of the world some might be decorated with shells, tusks or teeth of animals, with seeds, leaves or beads. The latter might have been trade gifts from Westerners. African masks carved from wood had a great influence on Picasso.

## TOTEM POLES

Totem poles, carved from single tree trunks, some as high as 27 metres, were full of beautiful carvings - and were made for specific purposes. The North American Indian chieftains would put them outside their houses to show the spirits of their ancestors - maybe eagles, bears, beavers and whales. The American Indians believed that animals and humans and nature were closely linked - perhaps the ancestor of a particular clan had been an eagle. Other animals maybe became important symbols for them because an ancestor had once been saved by a bear. These carvings represented the spirits which protected the tribe. Many American Indians still use animal symbols today.

## CARVINGS ON HOMES AND BOATS

The Maori people in New Zealand, like many others throughout the world, carved designs on their ceremonial buildings, their canoes and their homes. A large relief carving of a menacing ancestral figure holding a club, with its tongue sticking out of its open mouth, gives protection from outsiders. Some Maori carvings look weirdly similar to pictures on ancient Chinese dings (see p32) - these were made in China before New Zealand was even populated. Could they be connected? There is a theory in the body painting section below ...

## BARK PAINTING

Painting pieces of bark has a long tradition in Australia and is still carried out by Aborigines in some parts of Australia today.

There has been a great revival in general in Aboriginal style paintings in Australia and in the knowledge and understanding of the symbols used in them. For example, in Central Australian paintings, "wavy lines" across a piece of work usually represent water or rain, while "a circle within a circle, within a circle" can be a waterhole, for example.

## Body Painting

Body painting and tattooing has been practised by many cultures for thousands of years and is still practised in the South Pacific. A frozen grave opened in the Altai Mountains in the 1940s  revealed a 2,500 year-old man who had tattoos on his body! Body painting is probably one of the oldest arts of mankind. It lasts only a single lifetime, but the traditional styles and patterns and significance get passed on from generation to generation. There is a theory that this is how modern Maori carvings in New Zealand have a similarity to Chinese carvings 3,000 years ago!

"Tattoo" is actually a Polynesian word for body painting! It was introduced into European languages in the late 18th century when Europeans first visited these islands.

It was the same grave that the oldest Persian carpet in the world was found! - see p34.

# OLIVE AND ANDY'S FINAL PAINT SPLODGE!

*Remember*: you can never separate what you see from what you know - when you look at a piece of art all the things you know have an influence on what you might think about it.

For example, something in it might remind you of your house, or there might be a symbol that you understand - even if it isn't one from your culture. An example is the way the Sydney Opera House roof looks like sails. If you had never seen a sail you would probably think of something else when you looked at it, something from your own experience.

Now you've read this book, knowing what different artists in different times have done will influence your reaction too. You might also think "What is the artist's purpose?" or "Why did he or she use those colours?".

Keep looking and keep thinking!

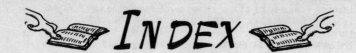

# INDEX

# NOW READ ON

If you want to find out more about art and art history, see if your local library or bookshop has these books:

WHAT IS ART?
By Rosemary Davidson (Oxford University Press, 1993). This book asks and answers lots of questions about art and has pictures from many different times, places and cultures (including *Children's Games*, see page 61).

MAGIC IN ART
By Alexander Sturgis (Belitha Press, UK, 1996). An amusing, interesting and informative look at illusions and tricks that artists have used through the ages.

THE ART BOOK
(Phaidon Press, 1996). As it says in the book's introduction, "this is an A-Z of 500 great painters and sculptors from medieval to modern times". Each artist mentioned has a full-page colour picture of a typical work, with some words about the artist and the image portrayed.

THE STORY OF ART
By E.H. Gombrich (Phaidon Press, 1995). This book is an overview of world art from cave paintings to the modern day and has a picture of every piece of work - painting, sculpture or piece of architecture - that the author discusses.

# WHERE TO SEE "ART"

Local museums and art galleries will always have examples of art which (as you now know!) can range from paintings by 20th century artists to examples of ancient pottery and jewellery. Some pieces might be by someone famous, while others might be by local artists. Look in your library for details of places to go where you live. Also check to see if there is any interesting architecture near you ... or a statue which has an unusual story behind it.

If you have the chance to go further afield, some of the larger museums and galleries are:

## UK & REPUBLIC OF IRELAND
BELFAST: Ulster Museum
CARDIFF: National Museum of Wales
DUBLIN: The National Gallery of Ireland
EDINBURGH: National Gallery of Scotland
GLASGOW: The Burrell Collection
LEEDS: Leeds City Art Gallery
LONDON: British Museum, National Gallery, Tate Gallery, Victoria and Albert Museum
MANCHESTER: Manchester City Art Gallery

## AUSTRALIA
ADELAIDE: Tandanya (Aboriginal art)
CANBERRA: The National Gallery of Australia
SYDNEY: The Museum of Contemporary Art, The Art Gallery of New South Wales

# ABOUT THE AUTHOR

Catherine Charley is a writer and teacher. She is interested in *everything* and loves writing information books for children because it gives her an excuse to spend lots of time researching into fascinating subject areas!

Catherine studied History at Edinburgh University and during her varied career since then has worked in television, radio, marketing and public relations.

She has travelled to many parts of the world and even lived in China for two years where she taught History and English at Beijing Foreign Studies University. She now lives in Northern Ireland but still travels widely.

Although Catherine herself can't draw, other members of her family can - and her great-great-aunt, Helen Brett, was a particularly talented artist.

## OTHER BOOKS IN THIS SERIES